Restoration

Restoration is set in eighteenth-century England: a world of cruelty, injustice and iron privilege. Lord Are is forced by poverty into an unwanted marriage with the daughter of a wealthy mineowner. One morning, during breakfast, he commits a bizarre and fatal crime. He seeks to pin responsibility for it on his guileless, illiterate footman, Bob Hedges. A battle ensues between Bob's black, justice-hungry wife and the fortified privilege of the ruling classes.

'Edward Bond's *Restoration* tower like a colossus . . . its stylistic wit, moral complexity and theatrical force are of the kind one associates with classic drama'
Michael Billington, *Guardian*

'Bond's great gift as a comic moralist makes Lord Are condemn himself without sacrificing a scintilla of wit. Bond takes the Restoration style, enters it and turns it against itself ' Robet Cushman, *Observer*

by the same author

A-A-AMERICA!
(Grandma Faust, The Swing)
AT THE INLAND SEA
THE CHILDREN & HAVE I NONE
COFFEE
THE CRIME OF THE TWENTY-FIRST CENTURY
ELEVEN VESTS
HUMAN CANNON
LEAR
OLLY'S PRISON
SAVED
THE SEA
TUESDAY
TWO POST-MODERN PLAYS
(Jackets, In the Company of Men *with* September)
THE WAR PLAYS
(Red Black and Ignorant, The Tin Can Poeple, Great Peace)

PLAYS: ONE
(Saved, Early Morning, The Pope's Wedding)
PLAYS: TWO
(Lear, The Sea, Narrow Road to the Deep North,
Black Mass, Passion)
PLAYS: THREE
(Bingo, The Fool, The Woman *with* Stone)
PLAYS: FOUR
(The Worlds *with* The Activists Papers, Restoration, Summer)
PLAYS: FIVE
(Human Cannon, The Bundle,
Jackets, In the Company of Men)
PLAYS: SIX
(The War Plays, Choruses from After the Assassinations)

Poetry
THEATRE POEMS AND SONGS
POEMS 1978–1985

Non-fiction
THE HIDDEN PLOT: NOTES ON THEATRE AND THE STATE
SELECTIONS FROM THE NOTEBOOKS OF EDWARD BOND: VOL. I 1959–1980
SELECTIONS FROM THE NOTEBOOKS OF EDWARD BOND: VOL. II 1980–1995

also available
translated by Edward Bond and
Elisabeth Bond-Pablé

WEDEKIND PLAYS: ONE
(Spring Awakening, Lulu: A Monster Tragedy)

Edward Bond

Restoration

A Pastoral

METHUEN

Methuen 2000

3 5 7 9 10 8 6 4

First published in Great Britain in 1981 in the Royal Court Writers
series by Eyre Methuen Ltd.
Revised and re-set in 1982 in the Methuen Modern Plays
series by Methuen London Ltd.

Revised in 1992 for *Edward Bond Plays: 4*
published by Methuen Drama.

This edition published in 2000 by Methuen Publishing Limited,
215 Vauxhall Bridge Road, London SW1V 1EJ.

Methuen Publishing Limited Reg. No. 3543167

A CIP catalogue record for this book
is available from the British Library

ISBN 0 413 76030 8

Printed and bound in Great Britain by
Cox & Wyman Ltd, Reading, Berkshire

Caution

Restoration

A Pastoral

Restoration was first presented at the Royal Court Theatre, London on 21 July 1981, with the following cast:

BOB	Philip Davis
LORD ARE	Simon Callow
FRANK	Nicholas Ball
MR HARDACHE	Wolfe Morris
PARSON	Norman Tyrrell
GABRIEL	John Barrett
MESSENGER	Kit Jackson
GAOLER	Patrick Murray
ROSE	Debbie Bishop
MOTHER, *Mrs Hedges*	Elizabeth Bradley
ANN	Eva Griffith
MRS WILSON	Darlene Johnson
OLD LADY ARE	Irene Handl

Directed by Edward Bond
Music by Nick Bicât
Designed by Hayden Griffin and Gemma Jackson
Lighting by Rory Dempster

England, eighteenth century – or another place at another time

Part One

Part Two

Note on the songs

In the first production of *Restoration* 'Hurrah' was cut from Scene Eight. It would be possible to cut 'Dream Song' from Scene Eleven and sing it between Scenes Ten and Eleven. 'Suddenly' would then have to be cut.

It's a Big Broad Fine Sunny Day

It's a big broad fine sunny day
The black clouds are gonna blow away
It's true that the rockets are aimed in their pits
But they wont be fired, not this time
This time there ain't gonna be any crime
This time we're gonna say no
This time we're gonna be wise guys
And tell the bastards where to go

It's a big broad fine sunny day
It's getting more sunny all the time
It's true that the bombs are stacked in their racks
But we won't load them up, not this time
This time there ain't gonna be no more war
This time we're gonna say no
This time we're gonna be wise guys
And tell the bastards where to go

It's a big broad fine sunny day
It's getting better all the time
And this time the soldiers will not march away
So they won't be shot at, not this time
This time they ain't gonna die for the sods
This time they're gonna say no
This time they're staying here to play
And tell the bastards where to go

It's a big broad fine sunny day
And the sky gets bluer all the time
From now on we'll live in the way that we say
And we won't be told, not this time
This is our world and it's staying that way
This time we're gonna say no
Today we'll live till tomorrow
And tell the bastards where to go

Part One

Scene One

London.
The Park of LORD ARE's *house.*
ARE *and* FRANK. FRANK *is in livery.*

ARE. Lean me against that great thing.

FRANK. The oak sir?

ARE. Hold your tongue. No no! D'ye want me to appear drunk? Nonchalant. As if I often spent the day leaning against an oak or supine in the grass.

FRANK. Your lordship comfortable?

ARE. No scab I am not, if that gives ye joy. Hang my scarf over the twig. Delicately! – as if some discriminating wind had cast it there. Stand off. How do I look?

FRANK. Well sir ... how would yer like to look?

ARE. I wore my russet and green of a purpose. Must I sprout berries before I am at home in the landscape?

FRANK. Not seen your lordship –

ARE. Pox! ye city vermin can't tell the difference between a haystack and a chimney stack. Wha-ha! I must not laugh, it'll spoil my pose. Damn! the sketch shows a flower. 'Tis too late for the shops, I must have one from the ground.

FRANK. What kind sir?

ARE. Rip up that pesky little thing on the path. That'll teach it to grow where gentlemen walk. (FRANK *offers the flower.*) Smell it! If it smells too reprehensible cast it aside. I hate the gross odours the country gives off. 'Tis always in a sweat! Compare me to the sketch.

FRANK (*checks sketch*). Leg a bit more out.

ARE. Lawd I shall be crippled. *Do* they stand about the country so? When I pass the boundaries of the town I lower the blinds in mourning and never go out on my estate for fear of the beasts.

FRANK. Cows aren't beasts sir.

ARE. The peasants sirrah. Don't mar the sketch with your great thumbs. I had it drew up by a man renowned for his landscapes to show me how a gentleman drapes himself across his fields. That I call a proper use for art. The book oaf! Well sirrah open it! Must I gaze on the cover as if I wondered what manner of thing I held in my hand?

FRANK. Any page sir?

ARE. The blanker the better. (*Looks at the page.*) Turn sir. The poet spilt his ink and scribbled to use it up before it dried. A poem should be well cut and fit the page neatly as if it were written by your tailor. The secret of literary style lies in the margins. Now *that* sir could only have been written by Lord Lester's tailor, whose favourite colour is woad. Turn me to something short. Your master is a man of epigrammatic wit. About your business. I must pine.

> FRANK *goes.*

What a poor gentleman I am! Town house and park, country house and land as far as the eye can see, they tell me – for I never look out, 'twould remind me how far off was the town – debts to honour a duke, and broke. So: a rich bride. Yonder, about to rise over the horizon like a pillar of smoke, is Mr Hardache, iron founder, ship builder, mine owner and meddler and merchant in men and much else that hath money in it. With his daughter, who must have a title and country estate to go with her fortune. Well marriages have been built on weaker foundations. The heart changes but pride does not. So here I am set, imitating the wild man of the woods. An extravagant gesture but I would have the gal love me at sight and be spared the tedium of courting an iron master's daughter. Faith boys what would one do: rattle a spoon in a tin mug and call it a serenade? Peace good soul! You have but to glance up from this bundle of tasteless moralising – the relief itself will bring rapture to thy face – and the slut's fate is sealed. I hope I am not to wait for a change in the season? I shall put out branches or turn white in a hoar frost.

BOB *enters.*

A swain wanders o'er the landscape.

BOB. Well London here I am! What strange sights I hev seen!

ARE. Why does the fool gawp so impertinently? Lawd it grins!

BOB. Mornin' my lord.

ARE. Gad it addresseth me! Oaf be off!

BOB. Ay sir, where to?

ARE. Where to? What care I where to? To hell! Wha-ha! (*Aside*.) Dear heart do not discommode thy complexion. A raw face is a countrified look but I would not have one even to gaze on the blazing of the bankruptcy court! Dear gad my foot is misplaced!

BOB (*aside*). Doo a London gentleman complain when his foot move? However do they git into bed – or out of it? – Shall us carry yoo sir?

ARE (*aside*). I am dealing with a harmless lunatic. The iron people have turned into the avenue. Soon we shall hear them clank. – Good fellow, take the run of my grounds. Go and play.

BOB (*aside*). This is a test Bob. Don't git caught out. (*Idea*.) Drat what a fool I am! That owd rag round your neck hev hitched yoo up in the bramble! Tell by the look on yoor face! I'll soon haul yoo out sir!

ARE (*pushing* BOB *away*). Off sir! Back to your bedlam!

BOB. Why sir 'tis Bob – come of age and sent up to serve as
yoor man, as laid down in the history of our estate: eldest
Hedges boy hev the right to serve his lord. Steward writ an'
say he were sendin' me up.

ARE (*aside*). This comes from opening a poetry book. –
Sirrah . . . ?

BOB. Bob sir. Or Robert Hedges.

ARE. Bob, yonder is a paddock. Go and graze.

BOB. Graze sir?

ARE. A country lad must know how to graze!

BOB (*aside*). I must learn their ways if I'm to survive. – Ay sir.

ARE. Then graze.

BOB (*shrugs. Aside*). I'll chew three stalks t' show willin'.
That'll hev to doo.

> BOB *goes.*

ARE. Yonder comes my money. (*Reads.*)

> HARDACHE *enters.*

HARDACHE. Lord Are.

ARE. La sir ye surprised me!

HARDACHE. My girl's back of the hedge, studyin' the shop
window. (*Calls.*) Come daughter, or his lordship'll think
you don't know your manners. A retiring lass.

ARE (*aside*). Good. Let her retire to the country and leave
London to me.

HARDACHE. You'll soon know her ways. Mind, she has a
temper – like her mother. That blessed woman ran my
shops like an empire. (*Calls.*) Pst! Come daughter. – She
has all the airs of a lady. Learned it from the customers.
Not that she works in the shop now, O no! Last week the
soup was cold. She hauls the cook in and rows her out in
front of the guests till she shakes like a dog being shown the

well. Anything she likes, she must have. Saw a carriage
with a new fancy way of panels – must have. A duchess
with diamonds in her hat – must have. Skrawky pet dog –
must have. Little black maid – one of them too. I don't
begrudge. She's all that's left of her mother to me, barrin' a
few shawls. That good woman worked all her life – till we
had a penny to spend on ourselves and tuppence to mend
the damage – and died at the counter with a slice of dinner
in her hand. We're a family sort of family –

ARE (*aside*). Lawd he'll quote me the jingles on his family
tomb-stones.

HARDACHE. – and I intend to make you part of us!

ARE (*aside*). Pox if I call him father!

ANN (*off*). Pst!

HARDACHE. You call my sweet?

ARE. Fetch her sir – (*Aside*.) ere the ivy grow o'er me.

HARDACHE (*calls*). I'll meet you halfway.

> ANN *comes on downstage and*
> HARDACHE *goes down to her*.

ARE. Not uncomely, but the neglect is beyond redemption!
Style cannot strike at any age like a conversion. Its rudi-
ments are learned in the nursery or never. That redness of
cheek might be had off a coster's barrow for ha'pence. But
I'll take her, as she comes with money.

HARDACHE. Well sweetheart? (*By her*.) Hussy you're fit for
nowt but an errand boy but you're my daughter and you'll
marry an earl.

ANN. But father! He's got four limbs and his wind. He could
last for years.

HARDACHE. Shan't I buy good stock?

ANN. O you are a fool father! Lucy married a count with gout
who lasted no more than three months. And Audrey's old
baron died of overeating in a year – and he was no trouble

while he were alive. He chased her round the bed but were too fat to catch her. She lost pounds and looked better after her marriage than she did before – and few girls can say as much!

HARDACHE. Come miss.

ANN. Even that ugly Mary Flint. Her father got her an earl of nowt but twenty-five. But he was so eaten up with the diseases he was born with and those he'd acquired – and mad, she had three doctors testify to him before she signed the settlement – that when they came into church the poor parson didn't know whether to turn to the marriage ceremony or the burial of the dead. He were right too: they'd no sooner left the church than they had to go back in for the internment. She went with the peeling and came back with the tolling. But what have you ever done for me father?

HARDACHE. Presently my lord!

ANN. Can't you find one in a wheel-chair or at least on a crutch, so a body might hope? Did you enquire if the family die young? No – you are a thoughtless man father. And what does it matter that he has land in the country? You know I abominate the place.

ARE. Pray unhitch me.

ANN. Can't we leave him to see if he hang?

HARDACHE (to ARE). My daughter's too well brought up to touch a gentleman's linen in public. (Releases ARE.) Now sir.

ARE. Servant ma'am.

ANN. Good day sir.

ARE. Let me show you the grounds. A few roses, a plantation, a pretty forest, the best kept wilderness, and a jungle in the hothouse. We will not bother with the water gardens – a puddle compared to the lakes of Hilgay!

ANN (aside). Perhaps he's prone to accidents. – Did the scarf wound you sir?

ARE. Wound! Fwa! when I take a toss out hunting the ground cracks.

ANN (*aside*). Well, best know the worst. He's still the first box at the play, eating out in great houses, orchestral balls. I'll be presented at court and dance with the prince the second time he asks – the first time I'll be in one of my pets and give him a great yawn.

ARE (*aside*). Cupid has lodged his shaft. I'll beat up my price and set her onto that old maker of cinders. That light in the eye of a slut or a countess is the true lust for money.

ARE *and* ANN *go.*

HARDACHE (*calls*). Rose! – You youngsters go and look at the flowers. I'll wait up at the house.

ROSE *comes in.*

Call me if the hussy runs off. He can fondle her hand and rub up against her – but nowt else.

ROSE. Yes sir.

HARDACHE *goes.* BOB *comes on. He has already met* ROSE.

BOB. Shall us follow?

ROSE. No.

BOB. Hev you notice the sky is gold? Knew the streets ont paved with it. If I was towd the sky was I ont believe that neither.

ROSE. The sun shines on the smoke.

BOB. Lawd. I'm Bob. What yoo called gal?

ROSE. Rose.

BOB. Will yoo show us London Rose?

ROSE. Won't get time for sightseein'.

BOB. Ont mind that, rather kip busy. But I intend to see the churches an' palaces an' docks an' markets. Whey-hay!

Rose if yoor lady an' my lord git wed, as yoo say, us'll see a
lot of each other, which us'll like. Make a bargain: yoo say
everytime I goo wrong.

ROSE. That'll keep me busy. You run up here to get away
from some poor cow carryin' your bastard.

BOB. Thass a lie! Ont ought a charge a chap with that!

ROSE. Keep yer shirt on.

BOB. Thass all right then, s'long as we know. – Look at the
way *they* go on! Could drive a cart between 'em. Treat a
Hilgay gal like that she'd reckon there was summat wrong
with her. I'll show yoo how that ought to be done. First yoo
take the gal's hand an' walk her up an' down. Bin a hard
week so she soon git tired an' goo a bit slow.

ROSE. She's not goin' too far. She might have to come back
on 'er own.

BOB. He's a thoughtful chap so he steer her to a bank an' pat
the grass. 'Take the weight off yoor feet gal'.

ROSE. No, I'm wearing my best dress.

BOB. Yoo hev t'say yes or I can't show yoo how to doo
it. 'Look' he say 'yoo're a pretty gal an' he give her a
(*Picks up* ARE's *flower.*) Lady's Smock. Then yoo give
him a kiss.

ROSE. Why?

BOB. You hev to!

ROSE. Why?

BOB. God yoo're a disconcertin' woman gal! Thass considered very rude in Hilgay. Yoo hev the flower, yoo hev
t'kiss – or thass bad luck for both parties for a whole year.
Ought to give us some luck Rose – (*Kisses her.*) on my first
day in London.

Roses (BOB)

I lay a red rose on your breast
A red rose on a dusky flower

It rises and falls in the scent of your mouth
Your breath is a breeze that blows
In the silent world where the ice walls tower
And melts the snows to sparkling streams
And brings the swallows home from the south ...
In the scent of your breath and from the rose
The petals open and fall apart
Scatter and lie upon your heart
And there I lay my head in repose
I kiss the petals
They stir and close
Close to the secret bud again
The bud in which are hidden away
The breezes of spring
The gentle rain
And the warmth of a summer's day

Scene Two

Hilgay.
The Hall.
Porch.
MOTHER *and* PARSON.

MOTHER. Upset yoo ont let 'em parade in a line. Ont often
git a bit of fun.
PARSON. Let them work – that's what his lordship would
wish to see.

    ARE *and* ANN *enter.*
    FRANK *goes in and out with boxes.*

ARE. Faw! The dust! Parson ye have emptied your graveyard
on my doorstep!
PARSON. My lord I shall pray for rain.

ARE *enters the house.*

ANN. Every bone in my body's broken. My stomach's changed places with my liver. (*To* FRANK.) Mind that box man!

PARSON. My lady welcome to Hilgay. We asked a blessing on the wedding –

ANN (*to* FRANK). Get them away from his feet!

PARSON. – and would gladly have held the service at St John's. His lordship's father was christened, married and buried there, as were –

ANN (*to* FRANK). Don't slam it man!

FRANK. 'S heavy.

ANN. So will my fist be round your chops!

MOTHER. M'lady, Mrs Hedges yoor housekeeper.

ANN. Make someone keep an eye on the carriage! Who are those ruffians loitering round the back?! Be off! They'll steal my new things!

BOB *comes on. His livery is the same as* FRANK'S.

PARSON. My lady the parish has had an outbreak of methodists! On Sunday I took the horses from their stalls and drove the fanatics through the lanes. 'Tis no boast to say that on Monday the beasts were so weary 'twas painful to lead them to the shafts.

ANN *goes in. The* PARSON *follows*

BOB. Ma.

MOTHER. Boy yoo look smart.

They can't embrace because BOB *is putting down a parcel.*

BOB. Keepin' well?

MOTHER. Gittin' by. Dad's out the back, brought him up to the house. She the sort a creature she looks like?

BOB. Yes if thass cow.

MOTHER. I can handle cows.

BOB. Tell dad I'll be out soon's I git his lordship straight.

BOB *goes in.* MOTHER *examines the luggage.*

MOTHER. Huh load of old stuff. Ont need that here.

ROSE *comes in.* MOTHER *straightens up and sees her.*

MOTHER. Eek!

ROSE. Mrs Hedges.

MOTHER. Thought the devil catch me pryin'. Give me a turn gal.

ROSE. I'm the lady's maid.

MOTHER. Ay. Heard the London servants was getting black. Sorry I shouted my dear. The house is my territory by right and conquest. What goo on outside come under the steward or head gardener – I ont responsible for their lawlessness. Mr Phelps is the parson when yoo goo to church – which yoo better had, doo they complain – an' the magistrate when yoo goo to court – which you better hadn't. Yoor regular duties come under her ladyship but anything relatin' to the runnin' of the house come under me: where yoo sit at table, upkeep of yoor room an' any set-to yoo hev with the servants – I'm the law, an' the mercy if yoo're lucky. That clear my pet? Disorder's unprofitable all round.

ROSE. Ta I like to know where I am.

MOTHER. Git her ladyship settled like a good gal and come down to my kitchen. Must be famished. (*Idea.*) Yoo ont eat special?

ROSE. No.

MOTHER. Jist as well cause we ont hev it. I'll find yoo summat tasty.

BOB *comes in and embraces* ROSE.

MOTHER. You two know each other.

ROSE. We're married Mrs Hedges.

MOTHER. Married? Well. (*Pause for thought.*) Black cow give milk same as white cow. They say black the grate an' the fire burn better. Still, god doo goo in for surprises. Hev a daughter-in-law! Well send a lad to London he's bound to come back different. Could hev got someone to write a letter. I'd hev got it read.

ROSE. Their weddin' kept us busy.

BOB. We're very happy ma.

MOTHER. They all are t' start with, otherwise they ont git married. Well. Us'll hev to –. Fancy hevin' a daughter! Take a minute to git use to! Need a double bed. I'll invite both on yoo to a glass of wine in my pantry. Settle her ladyship first. Don't want a paddy on her first day in the house.

ROSE. Let the cow wait. I haven't had five minutes with Bob all day.

FRANK *comes in.*

FRANK. Nobs gone up?

ROSE. Yeh.

FRANK. Dump ennit? Cruel to animals keepin' 'em here. All the trees look alike. Don't yer get lost? 'Fraid to stick me head out the winder 'case I can't find me way back. Do all right though! What's the talent like? Smart lad down from London, good looker, spin a yarn, knocked about a bit – what? Answer to a maiden's prayer. Yoo bin prayin' ma? 'Ere, yoo speak English or do animal imitations like Bob?

MOTHER. Mrs Hedges the housekeeper. Pleased to make yoor acquaintance Mr . . . ?

FRANK. Frank love, I dispense with the title: don't pull rank. All them bulls an' cows runnin' abaht in the altogether – gals must go round ready for it all the time. But I don't fancy them fields. Now a back alley's been the scene of many of my –

BOB. Pay no notice.

FRANK. Speaks English though don't she Bobby. Well sort of. She yer ma? Pleased to meet yer Mrs Hedges.

MOTHER. If they bought a donkey for its bray I could sell yoo to the lord mayor. Git all that stuff out my porch –

FRANK. Your ma gettin' at me Bobby?

MOTHER. – before we break our necks.

FRANK. Ask me, put it back on the coach. Don't see madam stickin' this caper.

MOTHER. Yoo jist git them cases –

FRANK. Not me Mrs Hedges. I'm the outdoor servant. Bob's indoors. I fetch an' carry outside – *an'* not all this junk. In London it's letters, presents done up in little boxes, pick up from the florists, or follow yer lady when she's shoppin'. If this was London an' his lordship stood on that line I'd have to clean the front of his boots an' Bobby'd have to clean the back.

Song of Learning (FRANK)

For fifty thousand years I lived in a shack
I learned that a shack is not a place to live in
For fifty thousand years I built mansions for men of wealth
That's how I learned to build a mansion for myself

For fifty thousand years I hammered and toiled
All that I made was taken away from my hands
For fifty thousand years I ran factories for men of wealth
That's how I learned to run a factory for myself

For fifty thousand years I waited at table
I learned to cook and how to unbottle the wine
For fifty thousand years I watched rich men tuck in like swine
From now on the food is gonna be mine

For fifty thousand years I printed their books
I learned how to read by looking over their shoulder
For fifty thousand years I built libraries for men of wealth
That's how I learned to write the books I need for myself

For fifty thousand years I fought in their wars
I died so often I learned how to survive
For fifty thousand years I fought battles to save their wealth
That's how I learned to know the enemy myself

For fifty thousand years I gave them my life
But in all that time they never learned how to live
For fifty thousand years I was governed by men of wealth
Now I have learned to make the laws I need for myself

I have known pain and bowed before beauty
Shared in joy and died in duty
Fifty thousand years I lived well
I learned how to blow up your hell

Scene Three

Hilgay.
The Hall.
LADY ARE's *Drawing Room.*
ANN *with a book.*

ANN. Last night I had a wonderful dream. We were walking
arm in arm. A perfect day. Suddenly rain bucketed down.
We sheltered under a tree. Wind howled in the branches –
and a bolt of lightning hit it. It crashed down, struck my
husband on the head and drove him straight into the
ground like a hammer striking a nail. He weren't there!
Vanished! Killed and buried at one blow! I wasn't even

brushed. Then the sun came out. Well it would, wouldn't it? And Lucy and Peg – my best school chums – rode up in a carriage sat on top of a great mountain of my luggage. And I'm whisked off to a gala given by royalty at Covent Garden for all the people to celebrate my release. Ee I was that happy!

ARE *comes in. He carries bills.* ANN *curtsies.*

ARE. If ye've crooked your ankle try cow liniment ma'am.

ANN (*aside*). I shan't be provoked.– O what a lovely thing!

ARE. What ma'am?

ANN. That jacket.

ARE. D'ye like it? My plum red. Ye begin to have taste.

ANN. And that other thing round your neck!

ARE. The cravat? Pox ma'am 'tis a disaster! Odious! My oaf of a man left it out and hid the rest. Had I been visiting anyone but your ladyship I'd have stayed in my room.

ANN. O no it's a picture!

ARE. Well insult me to my face. It but confirms that your tailor's bills are wasted on you. Pox ma'am, one of us must give up this damned foolish habit of followin' the fashion – and I'm damned sure it ain't me. I'll get something from the marriage! Ye have the title and may be thankful that unlike the fashion that has not changed in the last six hundred years and will not in the next. When my mother departed this house in haste she abandoned her wardrobe. Hitherto it was a supply for dusters but ye may sort out something to wrap in. Her taste was execrable but it will do for the servants.

ANN. Your lordship will tease.

ARE. Tease ma'am? I never tease about fashion. On that subject I am always serious – and correct. Well today ye're pleased to ogle me like an ape, but ye commonly find my society tedious –

ANN (*aside*). At last he's said something I agree with and I can't tell him.

ARE. – and as I never willingly discomfit a lady I'll relieve ye of it. I depart for London within the week to see to the refurbishments ordered to my house to console me at the time of my wedding. I told the designer the dining room should be apple green. He hath sent me a sample. If any apple were ever that colour Adam would not have been tempted and mankind would not have fallen. Next I asked for a crimson drawing room. 'Tis a modest wish. The rogue hath sent me a specimen of wincing pink – the colour of his cheeks when I kick him from the house.

ANN. O lawd sir why wait a week? I'll pack my things and we may be off –

ARE. 'Twas agreed ye spent six months in the country learning manners. A wholely optimistic time but a newly married man is fond and believes in miracles – as well he may. Six months. 'Tis not my fault the designer hath gone colour-blind in one. Ye stay.

ANN. But sir how can I learn manners here? What refinement can I get from a duck pond?

ARE. Try the parson's sister. But keep her off Deuteronomy. She once went to Bath. The visit was brief but she heard a concerto. She will hum ye the tune if ye ask her – and indeed, I believe, if ye do not. I assure ye that if in six months ye are totally transformed none will be more thankful than I.

ANN. Oh you pig! Pig!

> ANN *throws a book at him. He picks it up.*

ARE (*reads*). 'The Duchess of Winchelsea's Guide to Conduct with Notes on Presentation at Court and Selected Subjects for Polite Conversation with Examples of Repartee, Condolence and so forth.' I see ye have read it. Winchelsea is an illiterate hag whose conduct would have her expelled from a madhouse. Repartee? – no one talks to her but Lord Lester and his repartee is as sparkling as a judge passing sentence of death. Ho! ye have much to learn.

ANN. I'll learn you this my lad! Your title lasted six hundred years but it'll likely die with you! I shan't enter your bedroom till you can hear the singing at Covent Garden when the window's shut!

ARE. Fie ma'am! I intend to bequeath posterity the memorial of my life not some snot-nosed brat! If I have a boot or cape named after me – as I hope to have a hat – I shall be content. I tell ye ma'am, your father palmed me dud coin. I've had ladies swell for far less labour and far more pleasure.

ANN. You monster! You promised me –

ARE. Ma'am a gentleman will promise anything to avoid quarrelling in church with a parson.

ANN. Not his vows you ape! My vows! You promised me theatres, parties, dining in palaces, footmen, clothes. I was to meet the prince. I didn't expect you to keep all your promises. But you haven't kept one!

ARE. Why ma'am if a gentleman kept his promises society would fall apart. I promised? Forsooth and is that not enough? Have ye not had the pleasure of the promise? Your feet tapped when I promised you the opera! Your mouth watered when I promised you diamonds! Your knees shivered when I promised you the prince! What happiness I gave you! I denied you nothing. I was a prodigal of promise. Why ma'am have ye not noticed I promise all the time? I am a christian. I go about the world scattering promises on the suffering and destitute. Would ye have me hard-hearted and not promise my fellow man in his misery? Fwaw! Be silent ma'am! Ye asked to learn and ye shall. I promised! Ungrateful gal was that not enough but that now you must have the promises kept? What fool doesn't know that promises are better not kept? 'Tis plain folly in a gentleman to keep his word. I verily believe that is the cause of half the world's miseries. What surer way have we to drive our friends to despair? I shall not be so cruel to any man that it can ever be said I kept one promise I made him. Why I promise ye the stars! The Atlantic ocean! There is no limit to my generosity! I promise ye the moon! Now ma'am must I keep my promise? Do ye not know that every man who ever sighed has promised the moon to someone? Will ye all go a-squabbling for it? Ma'am I wonder that ye can live in this world at all with a mind so unschooled in polite society. The sundial is promised the sun – yet is content to read the shadows! And hath it not snowed in June? I shall now promise to pay your tailor and if he hath wit enough to thread a needle he'll know what that promise is worth.

    ARE *goes*.

ANN (*calls*). Rose! O I have a new purpose to go to London. *Revenge*. I'll shame him at the greatest soirée of the season. I'll wait till the prince, to further his cause with me, is about to offer him some high office and then say in a whisper loud enough to wake the postilions in the street 'Nay, sire, make him an admiral and your chance of a liaison is gone' then sit back and watch him cry in some magnificent palace.

    ROSE *comes in*.

ANN. Can you do voodoo?
ROSE. Voodoo?
ANN (*indicating a jewel*). I'll give you my pin.
ROSE. No ma'am.
ANN. O you heartless brazen liar! I'm sure your mother

taught you. It comes naturally to you people. You cut a
chicken's neck and say spells.

ROSE. I don't believe in all that.

ANN. If only someone would help me! I tried sticking pins in
a doll when we were married. This house is haunted. A girl
was bricked up for carrying on out of wedlock. She comes
out of the wall of a morning and wails. I don't have to keep
you on when I get to London. Black girls aren't the novelty
they were Miss Will-when-she-wants-to. You're two a
penny. Rose you could dress up as the ghost and threaten
him.

ROSE. My husband wouldn't let me.

ANN. We shan't tell him.

ROSE. If his lordship found out he'd sack me and my
husband.

ANN. Very well. You had your warning. I'll do it myself.

Dream (ROSE)

I sit in a boat and float down a river of fire
The boat is cool – it doesn't burn in the heat
The flames hide us from the banks
Where the whiteman aims his gun
The boat sails safely on
The whitemen rage and stamp their feet
Then the fire flows up the banks and into the trees
The whitemen run and the fire comes on
The river of fire chases them till they fall
To their knees and crawl about in the flames
The river burns everything that stands in its path
Forests and men all are consumed in its wrath
    I am black
    At night I pass through the land unseen
    Though you lie awake
    My smile is as sharp as the blade in my hand

But when the fire is spent
The ground is not scorched
The trees are not charred
The land is green in the morning dew
The cattle passed through the flames yet are not dead
Only the whiteman's bones are black
Lying by his burned out tanks
Now cattle graze the river banks
Men and women work in the fields
All that they grow they own
To be shared by old and young
In the evening they rest
And the song of freedom is sung
  I am black
  At night I pass through the land unseen
  Though you lie awake
  My smile is as sharp as the blade in my hand
  The venom does not kill the snake

Scene Four

Hilgay.
The Hall.
'The Thieving Scene'.
Workroom.
Chest and chairs.
MOTHER *and* ROSE.
MOTHER *cleans silver and* ROSE *sews.*

MOTHER. Ont lose things. Thass took. Knife an' fork. Be the
    devil to pay. Yoo can write it in my Loss Book so I ont hev
    to bother parson. Yoor mother alive gal?
ROSE. Yes. She was a slave. Her boss got rich and came to

England an their kids cried so they brought her with them.

FRANK *comes in dazed, exhausted and filthy. He drifts like a ghost and talks like a somnambulating child.*

MOTHER. Mornin' 'outside'. Don't mess in here, nough t' clean up.

FRANK. Bloody hole! In London yer work all hours but yer not an animal. More'n two parcels an' yer call a porter! But what am I here? Muck out the yard. Heave pig shit. Ashamed t' smell meself. If I got back to London I wouldn't get a job in this state. Never wash the muck off me hands. Like bein' branded! Night time I'm wore out. Creep into bed. If I had a bird I'd fall asleep on her. Fat chance of that! (*Without humour:*) Their fellas guard 'em with pitchforks. O Rosie I'm so tired I could cry. Why did we ever leave London?

MOTHER. Jist upset his-self.

ROSE (*cradles* FRANK's *head*). Hush.

He instantly falls asleep.

MOTHER. Yoo London folks are a proper laugh. Bit a hard work hev him cryin' like a babby.

ROSE. He's not used to workin' in the yard.

MOTHER. Git used, same's everyone else.

ROSE. He don't mind working with his hands but that's *all* he does now. Likes to use his brains. He's smart – aren't you Frank? (*Shakes him awake.*)

FRANK (*as if waking from a dream*). Hens cacklin'. Cows roarin'. Horses kickin'. Dogs snarlin'. Bloody great curs! Dogs in London sit on cushions an' say thanks when yer feed 'em. These bloody mastiffs 'd rip yer hand off. Me nerves are in shreds.

ROSE. Sit down.

FRANK (*sits in* ROSE's *chair*). Ta Rose. Yer a saint.

Wood Song (MOTHER)

The wooden cradle the wooden spoon
The wooden table the wooden bed
The wooden house the wooden beam
The wooden pulpit the wooden bench
The wooden hammer the wooden stair
The wooden gallows the wooden box
The iron chain the brass locks
The human toil the earthly span
These are the lot of everyman
The winds that drive the storms that blast
For everyman the die is cast
   All you who would resist your fate
   Strike now it is already late

MOTHER. My family polished this silver so long the pattern's
rub off. Mother say 'Fruits pluck and birds flown'. Her
mother an' her mother polished 'em in the winder to git the
best light. Howd 'em up an' see the colour of your eyes in
'em – then they're clean. Show the babbys their face upside
down in the spoon, turn it round an' they're the right way
up: one of the wonders of the world. Kip 'em quiet for
hours. Saw my face in that when I were a kid. Mother
say 'When yoor turn come, yoo clean 'em as good as
that gal'. She's bin in the churchyard twenty years. Wash
'em an' set 'em an' clean 'em after but ont eat off 'em
once.

ROSE. Use 'em tonight. Have a feast. I'll lay the table an' the
parson won't have to pray for yer.

MOTHER. Don't be cheeky. Bad 'nough clean 'em t' let
others make 'em dirty. What I want goo dirtyin' 'em meself
for? Food taste jist as good off mine.

   BOB *comes in.*

BOB. Parson's called.

MOTHER. Goo upstairs?

BOB. Yip. Says a prayer – an' then off up to see her ladyship.

MOTHER. Git his glass of wine out on the hall table. Allus set it ready. Old man his age need summat t' set him up.

MOTHER *goes out.*

BOB. Look at that lazy sod.

Takes some tape from the work-basket and begins to tie FRANK *to the chair at the ankles, knees and elbows.*

ROSE. What's that for?

BOB. Teach the lazy pig to sit.

ROSE. He's wore out. (*Helps* BOB *with the tying.*) Go easy. I have to account for every inch of that.

BOB. 'He's wore out'. So 'm I dooin' his work. Truss up lovely me old darlin'. There! Bet he's hevin' all sorts of dreams. Ont know whass in store.

FRANK *opens both eyes.*

FRANK. Bob. Undo me.

BOB. Ont fill the horse trough.

FRANK. Did. Buggers drunk it to cause a ruck. I'll fill it up again. Come on, don't get us into trouble.

BOB. Whass a matter boy? That old chair so fond of yoo it ont let yoo goo.

FRANK. Rose.

ROSE. He'll pay later.

BOB. Ho-ho a bit of hankypanky?

MOTHER *comes in.*

MOTHER. There. Thass set on the table with the saucer on top. Keep the flies out.

FRANK (*trying to stand*). Come on Bob. It's no joke.

BOB(*tickling*). Ickle-wickle piggy goo to market. Ickle-wickle piggy stay at home. This ickle piggy goo wee-wee-wee!

FRANK. Git off! Bloody lunatic! Don't muck abaht. Me foot hurts, the blood's cut off.

BOB. Whass the difference, yoo ont use it?

MOTHER. Spoon gone.

ROSE. Can't have. Count 'em.

MOTHER. Can't count. Tell it's gone by the pattern. Knife, fork – where's the spoon? Who's bin in?

FRANK. Well I'm clear. I was tied up and fast asleep.

MOTHER. Bob yoo ont got it?

BOB. No.

MOTHER. Rose? Hev to ask. It's my job. Easy git swep off by yoor skirt. Look in the pocket.

ROSE. Don't be daft.

MOTHER. Look.

ROSE (*looks*). No.

FRANK (*wriggles*). This is bloody stupid. Parson nipped in on his way up. Yer left it in the cupboard. (*Stands.*) Rose get this off.

MOTHER. Turn his pockets out.

FRANK. Now wait a minute! How could I do it? Trussed up like a chicken.

MOTHER. Could hev took it afore.

FRANK. Well I ain't.

MOTHER. Bob.

FRANK (*jerks*). Now look here. I'm not havin' this.

MOTHER. I'll hev to look.

FRANK. Don't accuse me Mrs Hedges. Yer didn't use that tone to them.

MOTHER. I know they ont took it –

FRANK. O do yer!

MOTHER. – and I'm me own judge a character. Ask to see in yoor pockets, yoo ont hide nothin' yoo ont make a fuss.

FRANK. You'd make a fuss if yer was bloody tied up. What yer do round here to prove yer innocent? Float in the pond?

MOTHER. I lose my silver I lose my job. Out that yard 'fore I turn round. Ont git another job with a bad name.

BOB. Hand it over.

FRANK. Look son – get this bloody chair off or I'll break every bone in yer –

BOB. All right I believe yoo: yoo ont took it.

FRANK. Ta. Now undo these bloody –

BOB. So we'll jist look in yoor pockets to satisfy ma.

FRANK (*tries hitting the chair on the floor*). This has bloody well gone –

ROSE. Let him go!

ROSE *tries to untie* FRANK. BOB *moves her aside*.

BOB. I'll settle this Rose.

FRANK. Keep off son! I warn yer! I'll bloody cripple yer! Treat me like an animal, I'll be one!

MOTHER. Grab him Bob! He ont got the strength to hurt a fly!

BOB. Us'll hev to see Frank.

FRANK. Look I didn't take it – an' what if I had? Thass my wages – by agreement. I get paid bugger all. Why? 'Cause in London I get tips. Take a letter get a tip. Keep yer wits open an' there's plenty of ways to pick up a bit on the side. All yer pick up here's the shit on yer boots!

BOB *tries to search* FRANK. FRANK *spins and tries to defend himself with the chair legs*. BOB *and* FRANK *fight*.

BOB. Quick mum.

BOB *grabs the chair and forces* FRANK *to sit*. FRANK *struggles and jerks*.

BOB. Ont help boy: truss up like a rabbit.

MOTHER *tries to search* FRANK.

MOTHER. Howd him steady! He's gooin' like –
FRANK. Bitch! I'll kick yer bloody – smash yer bloody –
MOTHER. Beast! Beast! Beast!
ROSE. Stop it! All of yer! Yer like kids.

ROSE *starts to untie* FRANK. *She releases his arm. He takes the spoon from his pocket and holds it out.*

FRANK. There's yer spoon. I hope it chokes yer.
MOTHER (*takes the spoon*). Any damage t' that chair make it worse.

FRANK *begins to untie himself.* ROSE *helps him. Suddenly* BOB *turns the chair upside down.* FRANK's *feet are in the air and his head is on the ground.* BOB *jerks the chair.*

BOB. Where yoo hid the rest?
FRANK. That's the lot. Crowd round here it's a wonder there's anythin' left to nick.

BOB *lets the chair fall flat on its back on the floor.* FRANK *again begins to untie himself.*

BOB. I'll search his loft.
MOTHER. Git Ronnie off the field an' tie him up proper. I'll tell his lordship we've bin thief-catchin'. Parson's happen lucky, so I ont hev to send out for a magistrate.
FRANK. Hold on. Yer got the spoon. That's the end of it.
MOTHER. Us'll tell boy.
ROSE. Don't be daft, mother. There's no harm done. Frank'll go and get the knife an' fork – (*To* FRANK.) an' everythin' else yer took – (*To* MOTHER.) an' yer can put it back. (*To* BOB.) Yer ruined my tape. Who's paying for that?

FRANK. It's just the knife an' fork – god's honest.

BOB. Us'll hev to tell.

ROSE. What's the good of that?

BOB. Ten't a question of good. Question of law. Ont break it us-self, an' if someone else do: we stay on the right side an' tell. 'S only way. He's been stealin' for years. Steal himself if it had any value.

MOTHER. Fine Christian I'd be turning him loose on my neighbours. He'd hev t'steal to live on the road.

FRANK. Yer have to steal in my job if yer wanna live. Yer fetch an' carry for 'em, pick 'em up, get 'em upstairs, put 'em to bed, clean up the spew. Stands to reason they drop anythin' – it's yourn. That's only right. Chriss! yer go through their pockets out of self-respect! Give it back, they'd drop it again or lose it gamblin'.

ROSE. For chrissake Bob. They hang yer for stealin'.

FRANK. Gawd.

MOTHER. Could of thought of that. If he was hungry I'd hev understood.

FRANK. Look forget it an' I'll scarper. Down the road an' yer'll never see me ugly mug again. Vanish. Now that's somethin' to look forward to eh? No hard feelings. (*Finishes untying himself, stands and offers his hand.*) Say cheerio ma? (*No response. Offers his hand to* BOB.) Come on old son. Don't upset Rose. She didn't know yer could be like this.

BOB. Ont trust yoo to goo through the gate: yoo'd nick it.

FRANK. Gawd you peasants drive a hard bargain. Stickin' pigs, twistin' necks, carvin' balls off calves – no wonder they treat people like animals. (*To* ROSE.) They after a cut? How much?

ROSE (*to* BOB). That lot can afford a bit of silver. Chriss the work they've got out of him, he deserves it.

MOTHER. Can't Rose, only do us a disservice.

ROSE. Please.

BOB. Yoo ont understand. I hev to take care of yoo now as well as ma.

FRANK. Gawd gal yer married a right little hypocrite there. Nasty little punk. Rotten little git. Arse-crawlin' little shit –

BOB. Thass enough of that before my mother.

> BOB *struggles with* FRANK. MOTHER *opens the lid of the chest and* FRANK *is bundled in.* BOB *closes and bolts the lid.*

Soon settled his hash.

FRANK (*inside*). It's a madhouse!

BOB. Yoo stay quiet an' think up a good excuse.

MOTHER. Phew he git me hot!

> FRANK *starts to kick and punch inside the chest.*

MOTHER. Ont yoo harm that chest boy! He's a proper vandal!

BOB (*aims a kick at the chest*). That ont help. Doo yoorself a mischief!

FRANK (*inside*). Rotten bastards!

BOB (*to* MOTHER). Git parson an I'll git the rope. Rose yoo wait outside, ont stay an' be contaminated by his filth.

FRANK (*inside*). Filthy rotten swine! Shit. Rotten sod. God rot yer yer bastard!

> BOB, MOTHER *and* ROSE *go.* FRANK *rattles the lid, trying to shake it open. Then he tries to knock off the end of the chest by kicking at it violently with both feet together.*

FRANK (*inside*): O gawd they'll hang me. (*Thump.*) Please. Why did I come to this madhouse? (*Thump.*) Please Bob. Bastard. (*Thump.*) Can't stand bein' shut up! Go off me head! (*Violent shower of footfalls on the end of the chest.*)

ROSE *has come in slowly. She stands and watches the chest.*

FRANK (*inside*). Can't breathe! Help! I'll die! (*Shakes the lid with his hands, then tramples his feet on the end of the chest.*) Never do it again pal. Promise. I learned my lesson. O please Bob.

> *Kicking and struggling, changing to regular thumping, and all the while he groans.* ROSE *goes to the chest and gently sits on it. Immediately* FRANK *is still.*

FRANK (*inside*). Bob? The spoon fell on the floor an' I was tempted. Honest. I know it's wrong but I –. No no, it's dark Bob, I'm confused. Listen. I'll tell the truth. I took it to get me own back see? You had yer head down tyin' me feet. I winked at Rose. She'll tell yer. O dear Bob yer fell for a trick there. We're gonna laugh. Come on old sport.

ROSE. Frank.

FRANK (*inside*). Rose.

ROSE. Listen carefully. Yer life depends on it. I'll let yer out –

FRANK (*inside*). O bless yer –

ROSE. – if yer do what I say. Hide in the yard in the little barn till it's dark. Then go. Stay off the road an' keep to the hedges. Yer –

FRANK (*inside*). No, I'll scarper as fast as I –

ROSE. Listen. If yer go on the road now yer'll git caught. Where's the knife an' fork?

FRANK (*inside*). Rose what if they search the –

ROSE. Promise or I won't let yer out.

FRANK (*inside*). Promise.

> ROSE *stands and unbolts the chest.* FRANK *opens the lid and steps out.*

FRANK. Yer darlin'!

ROSE. I'll get the stuff from yer loft.

FRANK. Keep it angel! I'll help meself!

> FRANK *grabs the rest of the silver, drops some, grabs it again but still leaves a few pieces.* ROSE *watches him.*

ROSE. O Frank.

> FRANK *runs out.* ROSE *shuts the chest, bolts it and sits on it.* BOB *comes in with a heavy rope. He goes to the chest and* ROSE *stands.*

BOB (*bangs the lid with the flat of his hand*). Gooin' to open yoor lid Frank. Yoo let me tie you up. No language – parson'll think thass Hebrew an' hev to look it up. Now then, git ready. (*Opens the lid.*) Ont git far.

ROSE. Yer like a stranger. I don't know yer.

BOB. Seem hard but it's for the best. Meddle in somethin' like this ruin yoor whole life. We think of us, can't afford to think of no one else. Hard times but we got jobs, we could be happy – but we ont if we meddle. He took the risk, now he hev to pay. Ont no way out of that.

Song of the Calf (BOB)

You take the calf to the slaughtering shed
It smells the sweat and blood and shit
It breaks its halter and runs through the lanes
The hollering men run after it

It snorts in the fresh clean morning air
It bellows and lows and tosses its head
And after it with sticks and ropes
Come the hollering men from the slaughtering shed

It reaches the town and runs through the streets
It tries to hide but the children shout
It turns at bay and trembles and groans
The hollering children have found it out

It scatters the mob and flees the town
It stops to rest in a quiet lane
Then peacefully strolls back home to its field
And enters the wooden gate again

And there stand the men from the slaughtering shed
In a circle with sticks and a halter and chain
They seize the calf and fetter it fast
And lead it back to the butcher again

For though it run and bellow and roar
The calf will be tied to the slaughterhouse door
The butcher will cut its throat with his knife
It will sink to its knees and bleed out its life

The morning is over, the work is done
You eat and drink and have your fun
The butcher is sharpening his knife today
Do you know – do you care – who will get away?

BOB. Best git started.

ROSE (*points*). He helped himself again.

BOB (*stares*). Rose yoo git us into terrible trouble.

ROSE. If yer catch him he'll tell – anythin' to get back at you.
Let's hope he gets away.

BOB. Well thass a rum un! I come to tie up a thief an I hev to
help him git off! (*Tugs the rope between his hands in bewilderment and frustration.*)

ROSE. He's hiding in the yard in the little barn. I'll take him
some grub later on. My mother told me what the slaves do.
The owners never search the backyards, go tearin' down
the road, even the dogs – glad to be off the chain. Some of
the overseers go mad – off their head – bound to if yer go
round with a whip all day – an' start killin' the blacks. One
or two a year, then one a month. Use the whip so it's legal –
well it may be against the law but the whites run that. So

the blacks scarper or wait till it's their turn. Yer didn't
know yer'd married all that. Me mother said stay quiet an'
wait for the chance: it'll come. Yer were all rushin' round
shoutin'. So I waited quietly – d'yer know, I felt happy? –
an' let him out.

BOB. Rose yoo scare me. Ont talk like that, ont even think it.
Yoo're one of us now, yoo hev to think like white folk. We
ont hev madmen with whips – 'less we step out a line an'
meddle: *then* they goo mad! From now on yoo be guided by
me.

ROSE. Take orders? No. I 'ave to take them from them, but
not from you.

BOB (*quietly*). Ont row. Yoo ont understand yoo'll hev to
accept an' thass that. Yoo're a soft gal Rose, too easy
touched: thass a canker.

ROSE. I can be as hard as you. But I won't do things I grew
up to hate.

BOB (*holds her*). Wish I ont married if thass only gooin' to
bring this sort of trouble. O Rose, Rose . . .

PARSON *comes in.*

BOB (*holding* ROSE). Beg pardon parson, wife's upset . . .
He's gone.

PARSON. Dear me.

BOB. Ont set the bolt proper. Shook loose. My fault. (*Steps
away from* ROSE.)

PARSON. Bob you cost your master dear. Get after him. Take
every horse and man from the fields. I accept responsibility. We have taken a viper to our bosom. A stranger who
does not love our ways. Pray he has led none of our flock
astray! Thank heavens there are hours of daylight before
us. Scour every road. (*To* MOTHER *as she comes in.*) Did I
spy my glass of madeira under its friendly blue saucer? If
you would be so kind. The excitement has parched my
throat. Bob take my horse too.

BOB. He took the rest of the silver.

MOTHER (*stares*). O the wicked man! (*Bursts into tears.*) My silver gone! I polished it for years! The wicked man! Wicked! (*She weeps and sobs the word 'wicked' as she crawls on the floor on her hands and knees, collecting the silver.*)

PARSON. There: see how the guilty afflict the innocent. This woman learns of a lifetime's wasted labour. The cherished things on which she lavished her affection are gone. How will she occupy the time she would have devoted to cleaning them? I cannot lend her a consoling book, she cannot read. And who is to say that in the hotness of pursuit fear has not triumphed over greed? Even now the loot may lie in the mud at the bottom of a ditch.

MOTHER (*weeping*). O parson don't say so!

PARSON. Or be hurled down a well, lost forever!

MOTHER. Whatever shall us do?

BOB. I'll take the men right out to Coppins Point. He'll hev made for the coach road.

PARSON. Ten commandments! That's all that are asked of us. One little law for each finger, to bring peace to the lord in his palace and the goodman in his cottage. Yet ten are too many. They live by one: self – and seek perdition. Are you confirmed my dear?

ROSE. Yes.

PARSON. A pity. O I rejoice in your salvation. But the darkness of this day would have been lightened by the conversion of a heathen in my own parish. O you mustn't think all Englishmen are rogues my dear. I assure you most are as upright and sensible as your dear husband. Well, I'll fetch the madeira. (*He goes.*)

Man Groans (ROSE *and* MOTHER)

The house is on fire
Dark figures wave from the roof!

Shall we fetch a ladder
Or light brands to burn down the rest of the street?

> You to whom the answer is easy
> Do not live in our time
> You have not visited our city
> You weep before you know who to pity
> Here a good deed may be a crime
> And a wrong be right
> To you who go in darkness we say
> It's not easy to know the light

A man sits hunched in a cell
People dance in the street
Shall we stretch our hands through the bars
Or run to the street and dance in triumph?

> You to whom etc.

A man groans in a ditch
We take off our coat
To cover the man in the ditch or give to the man who runs
away?

> You to whom etc.

Scene Five

Hilgay.
The Hall.
Breakfast Room.
Table set for breakfast. Two chairs.
ARE *reads a London newspaper.*

ARE. When I go to the city of light Hedges stays here in outer
darkness. Because my forebears had the lice combed from
their beards by yokels must I have my cravat ruined by

one? I shall – (*Stops short at what he reads in the paper.* ANN *comes in as a ghost.*) That damned little Lordling Lester! The ninth time he's squirted into print since my departure! Plague rot his little ermined soul! I'll rout that martinet at his capers and see –

He sees the ghost.

Why I'll put on last year's breeches! The family ghost! (*Puts down the paper.*) Mother I beg your pardon. I thought 'twas the gin when it grinned at ye through the windows.

ANN. Woe!

ARE. Be off with ye! Disturbin' a gentleman at his breakfast! (*Picks up his newspaper and shoos it.*) Shoo I say!

ANN. Hear me Lord Are!

ARE. Hear ye? What listen to an ague-ridden corpse! When I want news or advice I'll go to someone a damned sight livelier than thou art ma'am. When were you at court or the play? Ye gad! what d'ye know of fashion? I'll wear something a sight more sprightly to be buried in! It amazeth me ye are not ashamed to be seen so in modern times!

ANN. Thy poor wife!

ARE. My wife? What of my wife? (*Aside.*) Here's a to-do, discussin' me wife with a ghost – though the subject is fitting. Have ye come to tell me she's to join ye? I thank ye for the good news and bid ye be gone so I may celebrate in peace!

ANN (*aside*). The monster! – Thy wife must flee to London. Flee!

ARE. To London? Why?

ANN. She is with child. If 'tis born here 'tis forever cursed.

ARE. Forsooth? And who will bear the expense of a London lying in? Let the cow doctor child her, as he did all my family. A curse? Lawd 'twill curse me for cursing it with its mother! But 'tis to be hoped it's a sensible brat and will understand it was the she-cat or poverty – and his poor papa made the best of the bad bargain.

ANN (*aside*). O my London revenge! I'll smear the paint on his face in the royal presence! – Alas that noble woman!

ARE. If ye pity her go and keep her company. I am not so hard put that I must seek the society of a ghost. I tell ye this spirit: I had thought to have been too harsh with the slut, but if it's with brat I'm off tomorrow. Her morning sickness will be nauseous.

ANN (*aside*). I'll frighten the monster to death!

ANN *goes*.

ARE (*muttering to himself as he settles at the table and resumes his newspaper*). Damned impertinent she-spirit, to disturb a man outside calling hours. I see the editorial doth not advise us the ghosts are walking. 'Tis a good story – yet I cannot use it. I'd have the methodists roaring hymns at my door and asking to see my spirit. Still, the news gives a man relish to his breakfast. London! Blessed city! Our new Jerusalem! Soon my shadow shall fall on thy doorways, my sprightly foot ascend thy broad stairs, my melodious voice sound in thy tapestried halls. London London London thou art all! I thank thee spirit and shall drink thy health when I come to town.

ANN *comes in*.

ANN. Woe! Woe!

ARE. 'Tis intolerable! Have ye come to tell me the news was mistaken?

ANN. Thy poor wife. That dearest, loveliest creature, that paragon of –

ARE. Pox! If thy news is so great it brings thee from the grave twice then tell it!

ANN. If thy wife goes not to London thy wealth is lost!

ARE. This is arrant posturing! She hath raised thee to badger me. She stays. Go! I defy thee. (*Aside.*) 'Fore god I am taken with my style. Who'd have thought I'd unloose such a show of bravado?

ANN. Thy wife –

ARE. Stays.

ANN. Then curses on your ugly face! Your evil old –

ARE. I shall not have my face insulted at breakfast by a zombie!

ARE *goes*.

ANN. O the wretch! I'll poison him! No I'll poison myself and haunt him!

ARE *comes back with a drawn rapier*.

ARE. Out vapour! (*Whirls his rapier.*) I shall stir you up and blow you off in a mist!

ANN. O wretch!

ARE. It backs! What – ye remember cold steel? Have at ye! I would not be inhospitable to anyone but ye have a place: the wall – or anywhere at all of Lord Lester's. A man may breakfast at peace in his home before he's reminded there is religion – or it's not England!

ARE *runs* ANN *through*.

ANN. O. (*Falls.*)

ARE. Why 'tis a heavy ghost! I had thought to go whisk-whisk and – as I am a gentleman – opened the window for it and it had vanished in a puff of smoke. The ghost bleeds. (*Stoops, examines.*) 'Fore god 'tis flesh and blood. My wife. (*Steps back. His voice falls and he presses the index finger to the side of his mouth.*) Hsssssssssssssss ... here's a fine how-d'ye-do. My wife. Stretched out on the floor. With a hole in her breast. Before breakfast. How is a man to put a good face on that? An amendment is called for. It were a foolish figure I should cut. A buffoon. Murdered his wife. Got up as a ghost. Before breakfast. I break into cold sweat when I think of how I should use it had it befallen Lord Lester. I could not put my foot in a duke's door again. Never ascend the stairs to a hall blazing with chandeliers. Or ogle the ladies from the *balcon réservé* of a pump room. My life would be over. (*Nibbles toast.*) Cold. Faw! (*Puts toast down.*) A fine kettle of fish! (*Rings.*) Well you'd best sit at your husband's table. Hopefully 'twill look as if our quarrel had been less violent. Stretched out on the floor can only encourage the lowest surmises. (*Sets* ANN *in a chair.*) A man cannot think with his dead wife sprawled on the carpet. And I must think – after I've tired my brains with choosing a suit for the day.

BOB *comes in.*

ARE. Toast. This is as cold as a corpse – yea, and as hard as a tombstone.
BOB. That be all my lord?
ARE. For the moment.
BOB. Right my lord.

BOB *takes the toast rack from the table and goes.*

ARE. O thou Great Boob. Thou art my deliverer. Thou mayest be relied on. I do not see it yet, but thou art a loon and shall serve. (*Adjusts* ANN.) To arrange thee better. Faith thy silence is wonderful! Hadst thou behaved so when thou livst thou mightst have lived longer. Thy costume becomes thee. At last thy tailor hath done thee jus·

tice. Thy face had always a lowering look. You played death to the life. A performance to retire on.

ARE *goes.* BOB *comes in with toast in a silver rack, goes to the table and steals a cup of coffee. He sees* ANN. *He drops the toast.*

BOB. Eek! Lawd defend us! The dead are risen!

ARE *comes back.*

ARE. What man?

BOB (*points*). Th – th – th –

ARE. Ye have burned the toast? Twice in one morning!

BOB. No' – th' – no' – th' –

ARE. Is the child possessed?

BOB. Th' – *there*!

ARE (*goes to the chair and looks at* ANN). There is a ghost. O Robert thou art possessed! What have ye done?

BOB. Eek! A ghost!

ARE. How it spies at thee. It comes for thee Robert.

BOB (*sinks to his knees*). O no am I goin' to die? O lawd defend us!

ARE. What venom! Shut thine eyes Bob lest it ensnare thee.

BOB (*shuts his eyes*). Ah! Eek! Oo!

ARE. Take the rapier.

BOB. The –?

ARE. Beside thee. (ARE *kicks the rapier along the floor.*) Hold the handle as a cross.

BOB. Lawd! Lawd! (*One arm across his eyes, the rapier held out in the other hand.*) Mercy! Save us!

ARE *lifts* ANN *from behind.*

ARE. Robert! Robert! Take care! It advanceth at thee!

BOB (*peeps from under his arm*). Ah! O!

ARE *manipulates* ANN.

ARE. I struggle with it. It tears itself towards thee. God what strength! It will have ye!

BOB. No! No! No! No!

Terror! ARE *makes ghost sounds and lifts* ANN *towards* BOB. BOB *points the rapier.* ARE *leans* ANN *on the rapier's point.*

ARE. O Robert. Open your eyes.

BOB (*eyes covered*). Hev it gone? (*Uncovers eyes.*)

ARE. See! the ghost – the rapier – you: joined. Bob what have ye done? (*He pushes* ANN *with a finger: she topples.*) Murdered your mistress.

BOB. My mistress?

ARE. 'Tis – 'twas – she. I cannot say why she is so dressed. I do not recall she mentioned a fancy-dress breakfast. It seems unlikely. Who can fathom the mind of one suddenly raised to the peerage? Did she suppose society breakfasted in this extravagant fashion? We can never know. Impetuous Bob, how often have I warned ye?

BOB. Impetuous?

ARE. Certainly. Ye have murdered your mistress. Before breakfast. What greater proof of impetuosity?

BOB. But I – took it for a ghost!

ARE. As I say: impetuous Bob. I struggled with ye, but thou art a robust fellow and overcame me – and then, I had not breakfasted.

BOB. What have I done?

ARE. Murdered your mistress. Before breakfast. Pray do not stand there with your rapier dripping blood on my carpet. Hand it to me (*Takes the rapier.*) lest ye turn it against me –

BOB. Never my lord!

ARE. – in your present rashness. In one of your sudden fits. I see it now. A practical joke, a jape. Her ladyship ennuied by rural life – which must be said in her favour – tried thus to brighten our morning. But Bob you have no sense of humour.

BOB. No sir. I just do my job.

ARE. This morning you were overzealous. Well 'twas a paltry accident. Pick up the toast.

BOB (*picking up the toast*). What's to be done sir?

ARE. The future rests with the authorities – as it always does. (*Looks at a piece of toast.*) Blood. I shall not breakfast this morning. Forget the toast. One shudders at what you would do on your third attempt to bring it.

BOB. I begin to see what I hev done: I hev widowed my master.

ARE. Before breakfast. Few can say as much. I shall miss her pranks – this is presumably the last. Bob was I ever a bad master?

BOB. Thass what make it worse! Her poor ladyship.

ARE. Well she was not altogether without blame. Never play jokes on the servants. It agitates them into dropping the toast. That at least we have learned this morning. (*Rings.*)

BOB. What yoo dooin'?

ARE. We have a difficult road ahead. Turn to me at all times. I shall lead ye to the promised land. Hold no conference with others, who will mislead you.

BOB. Yes sir. I've made my mistake once. O thank yoo sir.

ARE. Do not fumble my hand Bob. Ye have slain my wife and I have completed my toilet.

    MOTHER *comes to the door.*

ARE. Mrs Hedges her ladyship is dead.

MOTHER. Beg pardin' sir?

ARE. Her ladyship is dead.

MOTHER. Dead?

ARE (*aside*). O the tedium of a tragedy: everything is said twice and then thrice.

MOTHER (*flatly*): Dead?

ARE (*aside*). Twice.

MOTHER (*flatly*): Dead!

BOB. Dead!

ARE (*aside*). I have survived the morning tolerably well, now I shall spoil it with a headache.

MOTHER (*suddenly realising*). Her ladyship is dead!

ARE (*aside*). If she is not she is a consummate actress.

MOTHER. Is her ladyship dead?

ARE (*aside*). O god is it to be put to the question? We shall have pamphlets issued on it. There are really no grounds for this aspersion on my swordsmanship.

MOTHER. Ah! Er! O! (*Weeps.*)

ARE (*aside*). Now the wailing and hallooing. Lungs of leather from coursing their dogs, throats like organ pipes from roaring their hymns. Well I have an immaculate excuse for retiring to my room, and as it cannot return I shall use it. – Mrs Hedges if ye have no pan on the fire pray run to the magistrate and tell him Bob has murdered his mistress. Before breakfast.

MOTHER. Eek! Murdered? Bob?

BOB. Alas!

ARE. (*aside*). And now the convulsions they learn at country dancing. – Mind, not parson Mrs Hedges. Captain Sludge. I could not endure parson's consolations on an empty stomach. (Bob throw the toast to the hens on your way to prison.) (BOB, *weeping, picks up the toast rack and nods.*) I shall have to contend with parson at the graveside. Sludge is a plain bluff man who made many fields sanguinary with the blood of his sovereign's foes. He won't set the windows rattling at the sight of one dead woman. Mrs Hedges to Captain Sludge.

BOB. Ought to give her ladyship a sheet. Ont decent lyin' there.

BOB *and* MOTHER *wail.*

Captain's is too far for mother in her state of aggravation. I'll hand meself in.

ARE. 'Tis handsome Bob, but I cannot let a murderer wander the fields. Superstition is rife: the hands would refuse to harvest. – Mrs Hedges the chimney tops will rattle down scattering fire and ash as if Hilgay were the sister city to Gomorrah. Your wailing will start the dogs, the dogs will start the cows, the cows will start the farm and so the next farm and the news of my wife's death will reach London by neighing and mooing. I would have it arrive by a more conventional conveyance. Bob wait. I'll send a man from the kennels. The dogs have been walked.

ARE *goes.*

BOB. If it weren't for his lordship I'd kill meself.

MOTHER. Don't talk so daft. (*She hits him.*) Put a brave face on it. Parson'll speak up for yoo if his lordship doo. Whole a Hilgay'll rally round. Yoo ont step out a line before – not till yoo married. An yoo married her in London (*She hits him.*) so it ont count. Why! if they had to find an ordinary chap they ont find one more ordinary than yoo boy.

Part Two

Scene Six

Peterborough.
Gaol.
Cell. Upstage door to another cell. ROSE *and* BOB. BOB *is
shackled to the floor.*

ROSE. What happened?

BOB. O I on't know.

ROSE. Let me help you.

BOB. Can't help. It'll be all right. (*He tries to comfort her but
she walks away.*)

ROSE. Show me what happened.

BOB (*half demonstrates*). I goo to the table. Toast. She's sat
there. Hands like so. Blood. (*Puts finger on chest*). Yell.
Lordship run in. Took howd of sword –

ROSE. Blood?

BOB. He tries to howd her. She howl. Stick sword out.
Open me eyes. (*Uncovers his face.*) Sword in her. Topples
down dead.

ROSE. Yer said there was blood on her before you stuck
her.

BOB (*confused*). Ont know. (*Shakes his head.*) 'S'n accident.

ROSE. They have accidents, we make mistakes.

ARE, PARSON *and* GAOLER *come in.*

ARE. Robert you bear up bravely.

BOB. Sir. Parson.

PARSON. Bless you. (*To* ROSE.) Bless you child.

ARE (*aside* to PARSON). This is a sorry sight: my livery in a cell. Cannot ye find him suitable clothes in the charity bundle?

> ARE *tips the* GAOLER. *He goes.*

PARSON. My lord. My sister shall attend to it.

BOB. We're jist tryin' to sort out what happened.

ARE. Bob Bob, why trouble your head with things that don't concern it? If I can't manage the affair as I see fit I may have to withdraw.

BOB. Ont do that sir.

ARE. I cannot be made a public lampoon. The good shepherd who found his sheep and lost it on the way home.

ROSE. Her ladyship was bleedin before –

ARE. Like a loyal wife your head is in as great a whirl as your husband's. (*Aside.*) The turnkey shall forbid her the cell. 'Tis seemly in a hanging.

ROSE (*to* PARSON). Her ladyship was sitting in the chair bleeding.

ARE. Bleeding? (*Aside.*) I repeat words like the rest!

FRANK. (*off*). Pleasure brought me to my end! What brought you, yer cantin' hypocrite?

ARE (*to* PARSON). My former footman. When we're finished here I'll go and rattle my cane through his bars.

BOB (*calls*). Ont hang. His lordship stand by me.

FRANK (*off*). Trust that fox an' yer deserve t' hang! Bang the door in his face! Yer no friend of mine Bob Hedges but I don't wish him on yer!

ARE. Don't heed him Bob. His present position don't qualify him to give advice.

ROSE. So she was bleedin' before Bob stabbed her.

PARSON (*shrugs*). Child the whole thing is beyond human –

ARE. Have ye never took a flower from a vase in the hall and stuck it in your coat as ye left the house? She sprinkled herself with paint on the way down as a final touch.

ROSE. We can see if there's paint on the sheet.

FRANK (*off*). Ask 'em to hang yer to music! Show the girl's yer fancy dancin' kicks!

ROSE. And the sword on the floor? How –

ARE. Mr Phelps next door.

PARSON. My lord?

ARE. We cannot let that fellow die with his soul in such neglect. For charity, go to him.

PARSON. Your lordship is a wonder! Even now I was silently praying I might be asked.

PARSON *goes out to fetch the* GAOLER.

ARE. Well miss?

ROSE. My husband didn't kill her.

BOB. (*quietly*). Bless you Rose. Yoo're the brave one here.

ARE. Bob –

BOB. She were bleedin' when I come in.

ARE. Let me consider. (*Goes to one side.*) The sun rose on the horizon – and fell back, and all the world is darkness. Courage good heart. If the sun goes from its course, why – bring it back. The oaf will hang and the truth with him. But it must be done quietly, and now the hussy will drag me in. Lester will scrawl me up on the wall of every jakes as a jack-in-the-box with a sword in its hand! 'Tis intolerable.

ROSE (*to* BOB). Does his lordship always eat breakfast with a sword?

ARE (*goes back to them*). Bob I must tell thee plainly thou art a trouble and deserve thy wife: yet I wish ye the same happy deliverance I had. What you or I say is no matter. Truth is what the lawyers say it is. You have none, whilst I . . .

(*Gesture*.) If Bob confesses, the killing is an accident. If he accuses me – well, have ye ever listened dumbfounded while ye contradicted yourself ten times in a minute? My lawyers will torment him till he runs to the scaffold – many an innocent man has willingly hanged to be rid of a lawyer. What if I go into the dock? 'Tis still an accident. But what a fool I must seem! Marrying the coalman's daughter blemished my name, but this – 'tis a scene from a farce. I cannot say why I did not know she was my wife. Had a kinder providence set the scene in a London salon, under two chandeliers, I'd have recognised her even with one of her father's buckets over her head. Would ye give evidence against me Bob. A lord dragged down by a working man? 'Tis against all civil order. Ye see the enormity of the thing? We are at the heart of the matter. In my person I am society, the symbol of authority, the figurehead of law and order. Make me a fool or a villain and the mob will dance in the street. If ye will be innocent, Bob, anarchy must triumph, your windows be broken, your mother's head cracked and your wife stoned for a blackamoor (He *takes* BOB *aside. His chain rattles*.) Come, we are Englishmen and may talk freely together. Ye have this chance to serve your country. Robert the Hero, hail! The nation asks it of ye. Stand trial. Be acquitted. I'll buy the jury. I withdraw while ye consider your reply.

The Gentleman (BOB *and* ROSE)
He steps out of the way to let her pass
On one arm she carries a child
In the other a battered case
With the hinges broken
Tied with a strap
He takes the child and holds it on his shoulder
He opens the gate to let the woman pass

He has not seen her till now
What politeness he shows the stranger!
In his hand there's a rifle
At the door to the gas chamber
He hands the child back to her arms

    Who would raise a whip when an order is obeyed?
    Why lift up your fist when a pointing finger will lead?
    Who would raise their voice when soft words will do my
        friend?
    Why use a knife when a smile makes cuts that bleed?
    When you have the mind why bother to chop off the
        head?
    When white hands will do the work why make your hands
        red?

    THE PARSON *returns with the* GAOLER. *The* GAOLER
    lets the PARSON *into the cell upstage. The* GAOLER
    lounges beside the open door and waits.

ROSE. The judge is staying at the Tabard. I'll go into –
BOB. Wait, we can't afford to make an enemy of him.
ROSE. He's guilty and you're innocent.
BOB. Yes but that ont seem t' matter. We accuse him we'll
    starve gal. Never git another job's long's we live. We jist
    hev to go along for the sake of appearance – like he say.
ROSE. Yer said yer always obey the law.
BOB. But he is the law – so I must obey him.
ROSE. But he's guilty and you're –
BOB (*head in hands*). Ont know what I ought t' do! Less think
    woman!
FRANK (*off*). Sold the silver and lived like a lord. Whored in
    the mornin', whored in the afternoon, whored in the eve-
    nin' when I weren't pissed!
ARE (*calls*). Confound it parson, pray to some effect!

FRANK (*off*). He's on his knees doin' his best, aren't yer old cock?

THE PARSON *comes in.*

PARSON. Patience sir. When they're to hang there's nothing to threaten them with. Not even hell. In this atheistical age they don't believe in it.

THE PARSON *goes back into the cell*

FRANK (*off*). Swillin' and screwin' till the landlord stopped me. Bastard knew me silver was runnin' out, just waitin' till the reward was bigger than what I had left. Slipped off in time. Lived in the fields. Robbed the churches.

PARSON (*off*). 'Tis not a confession, 'tis boasting.

FRANK (*off*). Jumped out the hedges onto the women and screwed 'em in the ditch! The last wild beast in England! I almost made London!

ARE (*to* ROSE). By the by, I brought the rapier in for Bob to polish.

FRANK (*off*). Open winder in Barnet. Put me hand in. Son of the house crep' up behind. Knock me out. Thick country lout. Drag back here. But it was worth it!

ARE (*calls*). Parson muzzle him with your cassock. – Robert my business presses.

BOB. A minute longer.

FRANK (*off*). Oi! is that Lord Arse?

PARSON (*off*). Purge his heart and still his tongue.

PARSON *runs out of the cell.* GAOLER *slams the door and locks it.*

FRANK. (*appears at the grill in the door*). Is that you Arsehole?

BOB (*to* ROSE): Least this way we got a chance.

ROSE. I won't keep quiet.

FRANK (*at grill*). Arsehole! I can smell yer! I thought it was the prison sewer! God rot yer, yer'll hang one day yer pox ridden rat!

BOB (*to* ROSE): I've said I did it, said sorry! They'd laugh in me face if I towd the truth now –

ROSE. If we don't it'll be too late.

FRANK (*at grill*). Arsehole!

ARE (*rattling his cane through the grill*). Fellow if your insults had any wit I'd stay to applaud. (*To* BOB:) Tis a great sadness but I see ye will stand on your own.

> ARE *goes to the door and is about to leave.* BOB *gestures to him to wait.*

FRANK (*at grill*). Arsehole! I thought my life had no more pleasure! It's worth hanging to call you cur to your face! I watched you lie in your vomit! Fool! I deserve to hang for not throttling you then!

BOB. It's according as your lordship wishes.

ARE. Good – you choose your protector well.

FRANK (*falls down*). Rot yer!

> *Sounds of raving.* GAOLER *opens the door of* FRANK's *cell.* PARSON *goes in and almost immediately comes out to shout at* ARE.

PARSON. Beware! Your lordship's adjacency brings on convulsions. He crawls upon his stomach on the floor. He'll die before scaffolding day!

> ARE *goes.*

BOB (*to* ROSE): I played the sheep, now I'll play the man. I'll git us through. Ont fret Rose. I'd rather hev yoor smile.

PARSON (*peers through the open door of the cell at* FRANK). A serpent or a great newt!

FRANK (*off*). Rot! Rot! Rot him!

PARSON (*running down stage*). Gaoler! Tis from Revelations!

FRANK *lurches into the cell. His hands are manacled. His leg chain pulls him short and he crashes to the floor.*

Song of Talking (BOB *and* FRANK)

My mate was a hard case
Worked beside me on the bench for years
Hardly said a word
Talking isn't easy
When the machines run
One day he dropped a coin
He unscrewed the safety rail to get it back
The press-hammer struck his head
He looked up at the roof and said
   The green hills by the sea
   Where the light shines
   Through tall dark pines
A minute later he was dead

Didn't speak even on the street
Once I saw him shopping with his wife
He only nodded
He was decent to me
But I'd heard rumours
He'd done time in chokey
And his fist could hit you like a steel-capped boot
Then he unscrewed the safety-rail
I nursed him on the concrete floor
He looked up at the roof and said
   The green hills by the sea
   In the dark grove
   I first made love
A minute later he was dead

You didn't pick a row with him
Once I bumped him on the parking lot

No real damage
He stared through his windscreen
Then drove off fast
A frown made him handsome
I never knew what team he supported
Then he unscrewed the safety-rail
I nursed him on the concrete floor
He looked up at the roof and said
   The green hills by the sea
   Where the gulls cry
   In the white sky
A minute later he was dead

My mates ran to fetch the nurse
The foreman wouldn't stop the machines
I bent to listen
He looked like an apprentice
He was gently crying
And babbling to himself
I touched his hand – no response
The hammer was still beating
I nursed him on the concrete floor
He looked up at the roof and said
   The green hills by the sea
   Through the tall dark trees
   The sea weaves
   A shining thread
A minute later he was dead

Scene Seven

Hilgay.
Copse.
Off, from time to time pig bells and pig grunts.
ROSE *and* GABRIEL, *the blind swineherd.*

ROSE. They found him guilty.

GABRIEL. He'll hang. Never seen my boy's face.

ROSE. Are killed her.

GABRIEL. Hev he any witness?

ROSE. No.

GABRIEL. Best howd yoor row . . . People allus fuss over what they can't mend. The whole world tip up an' everyone slid off – thass jist a saucer of spilt milk. Tell yoo what: know a sow's carryin' be the way her bell waddle. Another hev a great fat sound, thass time for the butcher. This job's all Sundays, like sit listenin' to bacon in the pan. Wife, roof, dry sty, eat an' sleep like an old boar.

ROSE. You talk Gabriel. Yer'd see if yer could. Even if it were jist ten minutes an' yer had to watch Bobby hang.

GABRIEL. Wrong gal. Ont hev it, ont want it. Sight's a curse laid on them who lead me, feed me, thatch the roof an' hang the door – life a sweat an' grind an' small pittance in the end. Better off sat in the sun, an' in the copse when it's hot. Ont bother no one. Break me cane, I git home feelin' 'long the trees. Whass the use of talkin' to neighbours? – could be winkin' in me face all I know. Got blind fightin' in France. Ont see the chap that took my sight – lookin' the other way at the time. After, they're all rejoicin' 'cause we won the war, an' I say: now what, can't work like this? – end up on street corner collectin' rain in me hat. Happen lucky, the old swineherd took it in his head to die an' I got took on at his job. Now where's the chap that hit me? Could a bin dead next day, fell off a ship, tree struck him. Who's to say what luck is? I hev the fruit of the world without its pains. Bar one. Mornin's – jist afore I wake – dream I hev me sight. Run up the hill, wave me arms an' holler at the sun. Then I wake up an' say: thass jist the boy left over in me. So I ont sneer at it – an' I ont weep. Yoo see before yoo a happy man.

MOTHER *comes in. She is out of breath.*

GABRIEL. What yoo all hot an' cross for mother?

MOTHER. She ont supposed to interfere with yoor work. Lose a pig there's all hell to pay. Whass she bin sayin'?

GABRIEL. Nothin'.

MOTHER. Hardache's up at the cottage. Push the door open with his stick an' say yoo wrote him. Sent him round the long way an' cut cross the fields. You let on whass gooin' on here, I'll cuss the day you wed my boy.

ROSE. He'll help Bob.

MOTHER. Ont need help.

ROSE. They'll hang him.

MOTHER. Ont talk such rot. No sense of proportion. This is his big chance. Doo his lordship a favour like this an' he's set up for life. Poor people can't afford to waste a chance like this, god know it ont come often. Time our luck change. Yoo start trouble, who pay? Us. Yoo're off to London, we git chuck out. End up at the workhouse. Work like a slave, workhouse disease – ont last six months, seen it afore. Too old to hev my life mess up. Look at him: come back from France an' got took on 's if he had twenty eyes. Could a cost his lordship no end of pig. He stood by him – like he doo Bob. So ont meddle Rose.

ROSE. Bob's in prison waitin' to –

MOTHER. Worse places outside. Ont expect his lordship to

goo in the dock for the like of her. Jist drag his family name through the mire. Whatever next! Ont know where to look next time I went to the village, they knew I work for someone like that. 'S'n accident *who* it was. Silly woman deserve to git killed. She come into my kitchen dress' up I give her a whack of my fryin' pan she ont git up from.

ROSE. He's hanged but the roof's over yer head.

MOTHER. You think I'm that sort of woman, my dear, thass yoor privilege.

ROSE. O I don't understand you people!

MOTHER. Jist ont stand in my boy's way when he hev his chance to goo up in the world. Lie on oath doo it help him, say I saw him run to fetch the sword.

ROSE. Why should Arseface help him? Bob's a labourer, no better than –

GABRIEL. Howd both yoor rows, yoo upset my pigs. The same thing if he kill her or not. (*Calls.*) Sibby! – If thass between him an' his boss, stand to reason who win. Drat pig! After them acorns at Pallin's End.

ROSE. It's not between Are and Bob. It's between two bosses.

MOTHER. Now whass she on about?

ROSE. When yer black, it pays t' know the law. You're not allowed t' benefit from your own crime. Are killed his wife – so he loses her money. It goes back to the next of kin: her father.

> HARDACHE *steps in. He fans his face, neck and inside his jacket with his hat.*

HARDACHE. Pretty place. Sorry I had to miss the funeral. A neighbour had to sell up and I couldn't miss the opportunity. Then the trial: had to arrange a little shares shenanigans. Rose, you married a villain but no one's perfect. All the bitterness was squeezed out of me long ago when my first warehouse went up on fire. Tell Bob I haven't wept since.

MOTHER. It was accidental Mr Hardache.

HARDACHE. Ay lass but some have accidents and some don't. Lads keep falling into my furnaces all the time. You'd think they did it on purpose. I see a furnace I go round it not in it. And if I saw a ghost I'd leave the room like any sensible man – unless it were me late wife.

MOTHER. That wicked gal's got it into her head my Bob didn't do it.

HARDACHE. Not do it? Is that right Rose? Then who did?

ROSE. Are.

HARDACHE. His lordship. Nay I've never heard the like. Happy young couple like that? Why ever should he be so rash? No, she were struck down by your overhasty young man, I can't believe otherwise – his lordship you say?

MOTHER. Yoo talk sense into her sir.

HARDACHE. Well I'm struck both ways sideways. What a predicament to fall into our laps – (*quickly correcting himself*) land on our heads. A real taramadiddle and no mistake. Did he strike her Rose?

ROSE. Yes sir and talked Bob into taking the blame.

HARDACHE. I shan't take kindly to bein' deceived Mrs Hedges. Now's the time to speak out. You know what's at stake: my daughter's memory. D'you know owt?

MOTHER. Well – I doo an' I don't. What should I say?

HARDACHE. The truth woman! It's a christian country, i'n't it?

MOTHER. Well – if his lordship kill her – what's the good of what I say?

HARDACHE. What good? Does justice count for nothing in these parts? When I think of that innocent young man – you did say he was innocent, Rose? – alone in his cell, my withers weren't more wrung for me own daughter. Well Mrs Hedges?

MOTHER. I suppose – if thass how it is – I hev to tell Mr Hardache that my son towd me he ont do it.

HARDACHE. And also testified that Are cajoled him into covering up his own crime. What a dastardly villain!

MOTHER (*finishing repeating his words*). . . . his own crime what a dastardly villain.

HARDACHE. Well. Now we know. I'm right glad I came to pay respects to my daughter's grave: you run into business anywhere.

ROSE. Mr Hardache you're our only friend.

HARDACHE. And you'll never have a better. Leave all to me lass. Mind, no speakin' out of turn. We must go careful if his lordship's acquired the habit of murder. Good day.

ROSE. Will yer go straight to the judges?

HARDACHE. Tch tch didn't I say leave all to me?

ROSE. I'll show you the quick way to the house.

HARDACHE *and* ROSE *go*.

GABRIEL. Gad woman! – if yoo was out a' doors yoo'd still let the roof fall on yoor hid!

MOTHER. Caught me between.

GABRIEL (*calls*). Sibby! Yoo git fat yoo jist make work for the butcher. – Gad woman them pigs talk more sense'n yoo.

Legend of Good Fortune (MOTHER)

Men lived in peace and plenty
When the world was as young as the day
But a god came down from heaven
And took the good things away

He put them all in a basket
And slowly climbed up to his cave
He put the basket under his head
And slept like a weary slave

There passed on earth ten ages of war
Men groaned and lived as the dead
When the dreaming god stirred in his sleep
And the basket fell out of his bed

Then from the heavens there rained on man
The gifts of plenty and peace
Bread and honey and fruit and wine
And the new golden age began

Slowly the god woke up from his sleep
And came down to rob again
This time men said what we have we shall keep!
And they fought till the god was slain

Send for the wise to share your bread
Take the beautiful into your bed
And if ever that god is seen in your land
Take all he's got – and break his head!

Scene Eight

Peterborough.
Holme Cottage. Kitchen.
Table. Chairs.
BOB *and* PARSON.
BOB's *legs are fettered. He scratches a pen on paper*

BOB. Hev a skill for learnin. Jist lack the opportunity afore.
   Hev a terrible struggle with my S. Drat squiggle of a letter.
   Letters is a miracle parson. Dance afoor yoor eyes an goo
   t'gither like a candle flarin up afore it die. Are say I'll be
   put in charge of clerkin. Scribe his bills. Chap born in a
   cottage ont hope t' rise so high.

PARSON. Bob do not set thy heart on a pardon. Seek salvation.

BOB. Ont be so glum parson. For the moment us hev t' make the best of a bad way.

MRS WILSON *comes in.*

WILSON. Dont splash your ink on my ceiling. Your mother's here, (*Gives* BOB *a duster.*) Wipe your manacles. Dont want visitors saying I dont keep you in a proper state. Look at my floor!

MRS WILSON *goes out.*

BOB (*annoyed as he puts down his pen and takes up the duster. He polishes his chains*). Drat! I was jist at grips with my S.

PARSON (*exasperated*). You are under sentence of death! Try to reap the benefit of that!

BOB (*polishing his chains*). 'S'natural yoo fret. Us understand how yoo feel, but it ont help. Come now ol' friend, ont like t' see you so depress. Cheer up an smile, doo us'll git cross.

PARSON (*aside*). The child's a simpleton. Lord Are promises a pardon to comfort him – and heaps coals of fire on his head!

BOB (*throws down duster*). Done! – In t' battle! (*Takes up pen.*) S's like a snake havin a tussle with itself which end's its hid an which its arse!

PARSON. Hedges put down that pen and listen! Our battle is with Satan. Bob – have you heard?

BOB. Ay parson, our battle with Satan. (*Aside as he puts down the pen.*) Us'll hev a sermon now. Rather hear the judge tell me he's booked me for hangin.

PARSON. What befell his lordship on that tragic morning – before breakfast, as he told the court – is not our business. I thought the London footman might don the halter. His lordship is adamant tis to be you. That is the situation we must live with. As god made water clear, you are innocent. But it is your duty to be hanged.

MRS WILSON comes in with a broom and sweeps round the feet of BOB and the PARSON.

PARSON. Lord Are is the guardian of our laws and orderer of our ways. Topple him from his mighty seat and Beelzebub will walk the lanes of Hilgay. Already the methodists rant at his lordship's hats!

BOB (*trying to concentrate*). . . . rant at his lordship's hats.

PARSON. There has been a murder and so there must be a hanging.

WILSON (*to BOB*). Up.

BOB raises his feet and MRS WILSON sweeps under them.

PARSON. Then the village will return to its ancient peace and Satan be shut in that darkness which – authority tells us – even his abominable fires cannot illuminate.

WILSON (*sweeping*). Winter coming but authority doesnt help me with the fuel bills.

PARSON. Bob thou art chosen *because* thou art innocent! Have ye not seen? – god always punishes the innocent and not the guilty! – that those in greatest need may be saved! For surely the bowels of the most hardened sinner will be moved by thy fate! In truth we are all sinners. Tis hard to follow in the footsteps of One who walks on water – there are no footprints to guide us.

BOB. . . . footprints to guide us.

PARSON. Be of good cheer! You are not the first man asked to die for his country – nor will you be the last. If you had seen the suffering of the wicked you would rejoice at your fate! Their rooms are little but they hold the empire of hell. For them I would gladly take your place on the scaffold. But I must protect the cloth, d'ye see? To desecrate this sober serge would be as impolitic as to loose his lordship's gaudy ribbons. You – though humble – are chosen in our stead! Bob! – pay attention. (BOB *starts*.) For now I must enter into theology.

BOB (*aside to* MRS WILSON). Take the kettle off Mrs Wilson. If he's in t' *that* us'll hev tea late.

PARSON. Your summary demise will atone for Adam's sin in Hilgay.

BOB (*aside to* MRS WILSON). An late supper by the sound on it.

PARSON. But Bob, the atonement you make for others does not weigh in the balance of your own sins. You see the theological quiddity of the thing! The lamb must be shriven before it's shorn. Repent! You cannot confess to murdering your mistress – not even *after* breakfast – but you lived long enough in London to assemble your own goodly collection of flaws! Purify thy heart! Soon you will enter the bosom of your lord. To enter that hallowed place you must be spotless! – Mrs Wilson cannot follow after you with her broom.

WILSON. I need a new one. The authorities dont provide that either.

MRS WILSON *goes out*.

PARSON. Repent! Christ would forgive you if you'd murdered a hundred Lady Ares!

BOB (*writing*). If I'd done that I shouldnt settle for salvation – I'd expect a reward!

PARSON. Bob have you followed what I've said?

BOB. Nope. I give up listenin weeks back. Jist cause a bloke's told he's t' hang everybody think they hev the right t' sermonize him. All that ol' quatch sound like the devil talkin backward – beggin yoor pardon parson. Jist leave me t' my book. Then I can read my pardon. (*Reads*) M-a-n-i-s-w-h-a-t-h-e-k-n-o-s-e. Kernosey?

PARSON. Knows! The k is silent and the e modulates! – how many more times? Those who dont pay attention in class come to a bad end! I should make you write it a hundred times. *Man is what he knows.*

BOB. Ask me the chap who invented writin ont know how t' spell.

PARSON (*aside*). Let us leave him to his book. If he go to heaven with a mind able to read god will see that I hath laboured in the vineyard to put some light into its natural darkness – though indeed this place is more like a tavern. (*Sigh.*) Alas we who help to carry the cross cannot be spared the spectacle of the crucifixion. I will call in at the church and comfort my knees on the cold chancel floor. His martyrdom will strike a blow against the methodists! I season my tears with gladness. (*To* BOB.) The silent k! (*Reads* BOB'S *book to him.*) 'Socrates: "He who loves wisdom obeys his country's laws with a gladsome heart!" and so saying he supped poison. Likewise "Man is what he knows".'

BOB. Was Socrates a writin man?

PARSON. His words were written down.

BOB. Us'll look him up when us git home.

PARSON (*sighs*). The Bible will meet thy needs. God spake the word and there was light. Man and woman to cleave unto him. And the birds and beasts of that ineffable garden. The stars in their firmament and the greater and lesser light. And the water that rolls on the bed of the sea. And the law of life. Look therefore that ye speak and teach wisely: for man is what he . . . (*Reflectively.*) kernosey.

MOTHER *comes in.*

BOB. Mother. Bear up old gal.

MOTHER. Bob.

They don't embrace because she must put down her shopping.

WILSON. Kettle's on.

MRS WILSON *goes out.*

BOB. Where's Rose?

MOTHER. Ont allowed in.

BOB. Why not?

MOTHER. Ont make the law.

BOB (*to* PARSON). Why not?

PARSON. Perhaps a regulation.

MOTHER. She's outside. (*Shrugs*.) Would come.

BOB (*goes to the door. Calls*). Rose! Rose!

PARSON. I'll go to her. Remember your promise: the best behaviour.

BOB. I want her here!

PARSON *goes.*

MOTHER. Well if thass all the welcome I git I'll goo home. Thought it'd blow over by now. Hev yoo back at yoor job.

Knocking on the ceiling.

BOB. Sod.

BOB *goes.* MOTHER *looks round in bewilderment and fatigue.* MRS WILSON *comes in with the tea things.*

WILSON. Where's Bob?

MOTHER (*looks at ceiling. Vaguely*). Knockin'.

WILSON. Mr Wilson, my husband. Sit down. You look worn out. (*Lays the table*.) I make him wash and brush his hair. Some of them lose interest towards the end. No trouble with his appetite. I cán't begrudge what I put on the plate. I'll be out of pocket. I was surprised how little Lord Are was willing to pay. It's so much nicer here than in the cells next door. (*Pours one cup of tea*.) If he gets off (O I'm sure he will) Mr Wilson loses his hanging money. This was supposed to make up the loss – which means it'll add to it.

MOTHER. Thankyoo.

WILSON. Mr Wilson's poorly. They say it's nothing but I know better. Those two are like father and son. Bob's propped his stick by the bed. Soon's he hears the rap he's up those stairs, rattling away. I don't say. D'you eat turf cakes? I made these little ones. There. I'm not the sort of person to count what they put on the plate. Five.

MOTHER. Thankyoo.

WILSON. His turns get worse. Passed the age for outside work. It's a holiday for them, but that's what it is for him.

BOB *comes in.*

Try not to clank dear. My head's been arguing with me all morning. We're down to three. I don't suppose we'll eat them all. Why didn't you offer your mother a chair you rude boy? I don't mind who uses them.

BOB *writes on a corner of the table.*

Mr Wilson says his assistant couldn't take a sweet out of a bag if you opened it first. We daren't give the job up, even I can't manage on what he makes next door. I like to have things round me, otherwise what is there to show? A change of curtains. Proper tea things but that lid's cracked. A carpet upstairs. A few pairs of Sunday gloves. They stick out a mile when everyone puts their hands up to pray. You feel a pauper if you haven't got a change of colour.

MOTHER. Thankyoo.

WILSON. I'll put the tin beside the plate. Then what we don't eat can jump back. Help yourself. (*She pushes the plate further away.*) They ought to bring it indoors. There's always talk but it comes to nothing. Out all weathers. Once

the ice was so thick on the rope they had to take turns in
breathing on it. Now Mr Wilson ties it under the horse's
belly to keep it warm. He's come home with the buttons
frozen to his coat. Had a dead cat thrown at him once. No
wonder he has turns. And the abuse if they fancy someone!
You'd think it was all done for his benefit. I tell him
'They'd know if they let them all off'. He said 'I think they
will next'. That was after the cat. Mind, there's two sides
isn't there? The better class tip. But you can't even rely on
them. One day they might just shake your hand. Even if I
know he's got a busy week ahead I can't say 'I'll go out and
buy that new teapot'. (*To* BOB.) What was it this time?

BOB (*writing*). Hand shook an' splash his shirt. Had to howd
his cup.

WILSON. O don't tell me he's having one of those. Eat your
turf cake.

BOB. Ont hungry.

WILSON. O a mood is it?

BOB. No.

WILSON. Don't have moods in my house. We set the cat on
them. Well when you ask it'll be gone. (*She eats his cake.*)

Knock on ceiling.

BOB. Drat! Forgot his Bible.

WILSON. What are our young people coming to? Fancy
forgetting a Bible! Under that chair. (*Calls.*) Bible's on its
way. – You are a funny lad at times. (*To* MOTHER.) It
occupies his mind when he's like this. He writes all the
births and baptisms and weddings in the front –

BOB goes out with the Bible.

– and his work in the back. Glues in extra pages. Goes
through them to soothe his mind. Reminds him of all sorts
of things he's forgotten. Memory plays funny tricks. I'll

clear away, there are light-fingered gentlemen around. I'll
wrap that cake with the bite in the side. I believe that was
you. It'll do for the way back.

MOTHER (*gently tugs* MRS WILSON's *sleeve*). His wife's outside. It preys on his mind.

MR HARDACHE *comes in*.

HARDACHE. Mrs Hedges. Ma'am. His lordship's here.

BOB *comes in*.

Say nothing Bob. I can read your face. A harmless prank
and you were the engine of fate. Here's half a guinea.

WILSON. Half a guinea.

BOB. Thanks. (*Gives it to* MOTHER.) Rose have that.

WILSON. Mr Hedges you're as thoughtless as my guests next
door. Now what have you got for tips?

LORD ARE *and* PARSON *come in*.

ARE. Bob, these are better –

BOB. Rose ont allowed in.

ARE. You'll see her soon.

BOB. Rather see her now. Goo back to the cell if thass
necessary.

ARE. Surly Bob, do not abuse my trust.

BOB. Ont hev her stood in the street.

ARE (*aside*). Well, move how he may it only tightens the rope.
– Ye make it deuced awkward for your friends Bob. I
broke regulations when I took you from your cell as
a pledge of your release. Let the blame fall on me
again. Fetch her parson. She was on the corner as we
passed.

PARSON *goes*.

BOB. Hev yoo my pardon sir? Let me see it.

ARE. I have it not on me, but 'tis safe. There's a style to these things Bob. The terror of the law, majesty of office and so forth. 'Tis not unknown for it to be held back till the man comes to the scaffold. Never lose hope. When you think the hangman is reaching for your neck he may be handing you your pardon.

HARDACHE (*taking* ARE *to one side*). We have a little business to settle.

ARE. What Mr Hardache?

HARDACHE. Your murder of my daughter.

ARE. Bob show your mother your letters. I'm having him taught his letters Mrs Hedges.

MOTHER. There! I shall hev a readin' an' writin' son. (MOTHER *and* BOB *sit at the table.*)

ARE (*to* HARDACHE). The Black Slut? – Father-in-law you did not build your empire by listening to trash.

HARDACHE. Wrong lad I listened to it very well. I call you lad because I notice you've started to call me father. I dont like interfering – but she was my daughter and she'd want the right man to hang.

BOB. I writ Rose. Parson can mix the letters up to spell eros – an' that, he say, is the lower form of love.

ARE (*calm and precise*). Why here at such a time?

HARDACHE. Where better? All parties to hand. If questions have to be asked they can answer them directly. And if you have to take lodgings in the prison next door – you're spared the extra journey.

ARE. Sir. My drinking companion the lord lieutenant – in whose bosom my hand lies deeper than ever the dearly beloved disciple's lay in christ's – will not let you clap me into gaol. Tomorrow I am promised for the races and twould quite spoil his party.

HARDACHE. Son-in-law. Your title gives you acquaintance, money gives me mine. I pay for the coach that takes your mighty friend to the races. Here's a riddle: why does a sensible man like me let his daughter marry a fop like you?

ARE. Fop? A fella don't boast but –

HARDACHE. Coal.

ARE. I misheard.

HARDACHE. No. Under your land.

ARE. I have been rooked.

HARDACHE. Your title cost me a packet but I meant to pay for it with your coal. The marriage made it mine. Or my grandson's – I think ahead for the good of the firm. The firm'ld do very nicely out of thee and me. Now this mishap upsets my grand scheme.

ARE. Why didn't my steward tell me I had coal?

HARDACHE. I paid him not to. But you can't have disloyal retainers round you, lad, so I sacked him on my way here and put my man in his place.

ARE. Father-in-law you are Father Satan.

HARDACHE. Ay well you meant that as flattery but happen when you know me better you'll think it's deserved. (*Document.*) Here's a simple agreement of intent. Our lawyers will work out the details later. All what's over your land is yours: that goes for the late Lady Are's money. What's under is mine: barrin' your ancestors' bones. Sign, and my daughter can sleep in peace for a very long time.

ARE. Bob lend me thy pen.

BOB. Expect a pardon look like that.

HARDACHE. Happen it does for some.

ARE (*signs*). This day I sign an alliance with the devil.

ROSE *comes in.* BOB *embraces her.*

BOB. Ont mind if the people see our joy, all's friends here.

MOTHER. Can't stay long Rose. Miss the cart back.

ROSE. Mr Hardache did you go to the court?

HARDACHE. Lass I considered it but it won't wear.

(ARE *leaves*. MOTHER *collects her things and goes to the door*.) You offer no evidence. Take my advice, keep mum. Bob can show me his pardon when it comes. I'll see he's set up in a good way.

Hurrah! (*All those on stage*)

When Englishmen owned half the world
All Englishmen were brave
And every Englishman was free
And cursed the foreign knave
Who meekly bowed to tyranny
When England ruled the mighty sea
All Englishmen learned at their mother's knee
That England was the home of liberty

Her prisons were houses for the dead
And on her gallows tree
The people hanged for stealing bread
Why steal when you are free?
They let him walk the streets in rags
Or dressed him up in soldier red
And taught him the service of the dead
Hurrah! for every Englishman is free
Old England is the home of liberty

They drove him to the factory like a slave
Or chained him like a beast
To crawl in darkness to his grave
His torments never cease
Till butchered in the wars of kings
His mutilated body sings
Hurrah! for every Englishman is free
Old England is the home of liberty

And so the generations go
Into the fire and into the woe

Into the trenches and into the blood
Bellowing shouts of brotherhood!
They break their brothers' bones when they are told
They think they walk in freedom? – they are sold
To the butcher!
They run to fetch the tackle and hook
They write their names in his invoice book
They whet the blade and hand the knife
They stretch their neck and give their life
Hurrah! for every Englishman is free
Old England is the home of Liberty

HARDACHE. Let's leave the youngsters to their peace.

All go except BOB *and* ROSE.

ROSE. Dog don't eat dog when they can fight over a bone.
  I'm going outside, climb on the wall of the gaol and shout
  'Are is a murderer'.
BOB. Rose he promise –
ROSE. He promised they wouldn't find you guilty.
BOB. He explained. Can't buy a whole jury. Look, old Lady
  Are was the king's whore or summat. Anyroad, she's got
  the pardon in the bag.
ROSE. Then why ain't you got it?
BOB. Can't jist hand em out. Hev to do things proper
  way.
ROSE. I've got money. We could get that chain off –
BOB (*removes fetter from leg*). Thass only for show.
ROSE. God! Then we can go! There's a fast coach to Lynn!
  We'll be on the boat tonight!
BOB. Thass madness! I git caught I git hang!
ROSE. You are caught!
BOB. What boat? Where to?
ROSE. Africa! Liberia!

BOB. What I do in the jungle?

ROSE. What I do here!

BOB. 'S different for men. Liberia! That where food grow on trees? Break a stone an' milk come out?

ROSE. Bob the door is open. The window's open. Step through it. If it was shut yer could kick it down. Yer could push the wall down. You're strong. You're a giant. But yer sit and wait to be hanged.

BOB. How I do love thee Rose. All ont lost yet. When I ont git a pardon, then I'll speak out!

ROSE. Too late.

BOB. I am an Englishman, a freeborn Englishman. I hev a right to speak – to shout for all to hear! Thass in our law. Stand up – in court, the street corner, top of the roof – an' shout the truth. It must be so!

ROSE. You're a slave but don't know it. My mother *saw* her chains, she's had marks on her wrists all her life. There are no signs on *you* till you're dead. How can yer fight for freedom when yer think you've got it? What happens to people like you? It's a circus! The clown kicks the mongrel and it licks his boots. He kicks it harder and it rolls on its back an' wags its tail – an' all the dogs laugh. Yer won't go, if there was a chance he'd put yer a mile underground an' chain yer to the wall. Then yer'd be free: yer'd know what you are.

ROSE *goes out*.

BOB. All my life I struggled. Bob the joker. Bob the sport. Walk down the road, the sun shines, eat, work – struggle to keep body and soul together. Yoo got yoor strength Bob, yoo can do anythin'. Where did I goo wrong? I know well enough. I know what yoo tell me now. Long ago I should hev put my boot in their teeth every time the bastards smiled at me. But I've left it late. Now it's dark. Black.

Black. Black. I must goo steady, or make a terrible blun-
der. I must trust the clown an' hope for my reward.

Song of the Conjuror (ROSE *and* BOB)

The conjuror tied his hands with an invisible rope
He bound his feet with a chain no one could see
He shut himself in a sack that was not there
And locked it with an invisible key
He hung from a hook over a deep dark lake
The people laughed as he struggled in the air
They stood in crowds to watch him twist and shake
With a fanfare he is free!

The conjuror was the idol of the people
He appeared at every festival in the land
He hung far over the top of every steeple
Turning and twisting and bobbing upside down
He struggled to get the invisible key
The people roared and laughed at his clever tricks
With a fanfare he is free!

One day when he turned in his invisible sack
He could not get free
He screamed like a man stretched on the rack
Which no one could see
His mouth was gagged with invisible rags
More more! roared the crowd and waved their flags
As he writhed in the air
And fought for his life in an unseen snare

They gasped as he fell – the splash
Turned the water white
They screamed as they watched him struggle and thrash
With horror they saw him sinking down
And stood on the bank to watch him drown

Scene Nine

London.
Old Lady Are's house.
Drawing Room.
ROSE *and* OLD LADY ARE.
OLD LADY ARE *in a chair. On the floor, across the room, a decanter.*

ROSE. They say my husband murdered your daughter-in-law.

LADY ARE. I shall send him a guinea. I never saw the slut. Her father hawked coals in Manchester and she trotted beside him calling his wares. A suitable training for one destined to converse with my son.

ROSE. My husband didn't kill her.

LADY ARE. D'you like fish? It lures me with the passion that drives youth to its follies. I ate too much at dinner. (*Points.*) My glass child. My maid Dorothea, the vixen, puts it out of my reach.

ROSE (*hands her the glass*). Your son killed her.

LADY ARE. My son? O I've slopped the glass! (*Chokes.*) Dear me. Thump my back child. (ROSE *pats her back.*) Thump I say! Lay on! O 'tis good! The seizure will take me. (*Wipes her eyes.*) Swear 'tis true! I must have my coach at dawn to tell the town.

ROSE. Thank you ma'am. I was afraid you wouldn't believe me.

LADY ARE. Believe ye? 'Tis the easiest thing to believe since the bishop of London's wife gave birth to a child with his chaplain's nose. I can't pay your husband – but you shall have the guinea.

ROSE. Lord Are says you've got us a pardon.

LADY ARE. Pox on the rogue! I haven't seen him since the day his father died. He snatched the pillow from under his head, bounded downstairs (one at a time, he had heels on), threw it at me, yowlped Hurrah! and hounded me from the house. (*Drinks.*) Come, see. (*Takes a huge pile of papers from her bosom.*) Shares, letters, promissory notes. All his. (*Wheezes as she fondles the papers.*) Look, forty thousand pounds. (*Paper.*) A half share in Jamaica. (*Paper.*) That would pay his pox pills. (*Paper.*) A castle in Scotland. (*Kisses papers and puts them back in her dress.*) Home to my heart, darlings. (*Paper.*) A letter from the Prime Minister to the Primate of England. You could blackmail him with this till he had to raise the income tax to pay you – and still have the Primate's reply. (*Paper.*) And this – a charge on his old foe Lester. (*Laughs and stuffs papers away.*) Back to the bosom that gave him suck (one Wednesday when the wet nurse was late) but now makes amends by making him starve. (*Smoothes her dress.*) They go with me to the grave and angels do not lie on softer down.

ROSE. He says the pardon's already –

LADY ARE. Pardon, pardon – cease with your pardons! My glass. There are no pardons.

ROSE. But you can get one?

LADY ARE. 'Tis true my figure sets a fashion few could follow – but the prince always liked a lady of carriage. He'd bed me still but his flesh is wore out with paint. His servants daub it on when they're drunk and he's too blind to wipe it off. Last week his whiskers were plastered to his cheeks with cold cream. They carry him round the palace in a sedan chair. He looks out of the window like a monkey sticking out of its jungle. A pardon? – nothing would be easier. 'Twould be as if the monkey reached up, plucked a banana from a tree and threw it into my lap. But I shall not ask.

ROSE. But Lady Are my husband's innocent!

LADY ARE. True, but he hath put out that he is not. Let him
hang for a boaster. Child, who would be safe? Charles my
footman would strangle me at table for the sake of a titbit
on my plate, Dorothea would crack me over the head with
my bottle and drink it, and Trevor my valet would kick me
downstairs. Pardon? Ye might as well ask me to lead a riot
or open a revolution.

ROSE. My husband is innocent.

LADY ARE. Then let him go to heaven. If he stays in this
world he will go to hell with the rest of the footmen. If
Society protest every time the law is an ass no one will
respect it. I've watched lambs as innocent as driven snow
go to the gallows and my head was not one hair the whiter.
Console yourself. My son will hang. Stab Lester at cards or
step on his toe at a hop. They'll brawl and one will be
stabbed and the other hanged.

ROSE. My husband is good and kind and –

LADY ARE. I like him more and more.

ROSE (*kneels*). I beg you.

LADY ARE. Get up child. A thing is not made more im-
pressive by being said by a dwarf. The ground is what we
have risen from. Up! Ye made an old lady merry with a
farce and now ye mar it with a wailing play!

ROSE. You bitch! I hope you fall downstairs! Choke! Die of
gin! Have your head cracked with a bottle! And get pox
from yer monkey!

    ROSE *goes*.

LADY ARE. The wretch hath a tongue on her like Dorothea,
but she would have stayed for the guinea. I forgot to get the
details! (*Calls*.) Dorothea! – Coupling with the kitchen boy
again? Trevor! – The wretch is drunk! Hush, I'll invent the
details. The papers said 'twas at table. She empties his

plate on his head, peas and potatoes stream down his face and French coat and he runs her through and slips on a pudding and turns cartwheels while she – O! Ho! Ha! (*Laughs and wheezes*.) her – her – O! I shall be in bed for a week! Peace think of something else! – her last breath blows bubbles in the soup! (*She laughs*.) O! Hoo! Ha! (*Stops*.) The cold wind round my heart ... The turbot. The doctor forbade it. (*Wipes her mouth*.) The cream sauce ... I am an old woman with an empty glass and there is nothing to think of that does not wring me with regret for the past, convulse me at the follies of the present, or make me tremble before what is to come. I have not always lived after the precepts. 'Twould do no harm to prepare for heaven. Pah! a morbid thought. 'Twould drive my son to distraction – that is heaven, and I shall be the *dea ex machina* in it. As in the old romances, he shall be reprieved at the tree. I shall send a copy direct to that scoundrel my son and give him the misery of reading it.

The Fair Tree of Liberty (ROSE *and* FRANK)

On the fair tree of liberty
The fruit weighs the branches to the ground
And look! the fruit are eyes
At the stealthy tread they open to see
The robber who comes to rob the tree
He turns around and runs
The eyes are brighter than a hundred suns

On the fair tree of liberty
The fruit weighs the branches to the ground
And look! the fruit are eyes
At the marching tread they open to see
The axeman who comes to fell the tree
He turns around and runs
The eyes are brighter than a hundred suns

On the fair tree of liberty
The fruit weighs the branches to the ground
And look! the fruit are eyes
At the heavy tread they open to see
The headsman who comes to burn the tree
He turns around and runs
The eyes are brighter than a thousand suns

Deep in the trunk bees murmur like thunder
High in the crown birds call
Telling the names of the passers-by
The eyes watch them as they come
And sometimes the branches rise and strike them down like
    bolts of thunder

And so the fair tree grows
As tall as the pine and strong as the oak
Wreathed with the climbing honeysuckle
The wild rose and the hanging vine
As our forefathers spoke

Scene Ten

Hilgay.
The Hall.
Breakfast Room.
ARE. *For the first time he is seen in a shirt and breeches and
without a wig.*

ARE. Let a man have a fine day for his hanging. 'Tis morose to
    say otherwise. An empty house, all gone for the best
    places. How pleasantly the sun shines in at my windows to
    bless me. This morning I asked after a noise. 'Twas a lark.

I would have sung too but I lacked an orchestra. Flowers nodded, lambs bleated. Peter Sigh the poet would have –

MOTHER *comes in.*

MOTHER. Gentleman.

ARE. Not so downcast Hedges. I tried. The law is a heavy stone for one man to move.

MOTHER. Say it's urgent.

ARE. Tell him no.

MOTHER. Hev a letter.

ARE. O let him deliver. 'Tis a small cloud, 'twill pass.

MOTHER *goes.*

Now to the business of the day: clothes. (*Sighs.*) A suit so sober it seems I shop at a monastery. I tell the truth: I shall be glad when the day is past, when those who are to suffer have suffered and the rest may enjoy themselves as the world desires, without the mournful countenance a christian must spoil his hat with on these occasions.

MOTHER *comes in with the* MESSENGER. *She goes.*

MESSENGER. My lord, your mother's compliments.

ARE. Damme the she-goat repents! The hag's at death's door!

MESSENGER. My lord, my commission is urgent.

The MESSENGER *hands* ARE *a document.* ARE *reads it.*

ARE. Handsome. So Bob has his good news at last. To think he lieth in his pains and I hold in my hand his absolute and perfect liberty. 'Tis feathers to a bird. How the affairs of men stand on their heads!

MESSENGER. I must go to the prison.

ARE. Prison?

MESSENGER. That is a copy. I am commissioned to hand the original to the governor.

ARE. So you are – or it would go badly with Bob. Lookee
there is a great crowd about the roads. I'll take thee in my
coach.
MESSENGER. 'Tis kind my lord, but I am commissioned to –
ARE. Commission the pox! Would ye deny me my pleasure?
MESSENGER. Yes sir. I am commissioned to take –
ARE. But now I think on't I cannot take ye. I have my Lady
Oxy to sit beside me and her mother the Duchess of Blare
to sit opposite and the Duchess will have Lucille her maid.
Now Lucille is an absolute termagant, an hysteric who
rules the Duchess with a rod of iron and will have no man
near her. The Duchess was on the point of saying I must
run behind and hang onto the strap. The maid compro-
mised only because 'twas a hanging. A wedding or thanksgiving and I should have wore out my shoe-leather pounding the rear. So ye see sir ye cannot come in my coach even
if there was room. (*He has poured two cups of coffee. He
hands one to the* MESSENGER *and drinks the other*.) No sir
do not ask: ye may *not* sit on the roof. That's booked by
Lady Oxy's boys and their chums – for the boys will go to
the hangings. We shall have such a hallooing and hurrah-
ing as we fly through the lanes, such a stamping of feet on
the roof, such a throwing of the coachman's hat into the
duckponds ('tis only a matter of lettin' 'em grow up before
we go to *their* hangin') (MESSENGER *laughs*) – that
Lucille will have hysterics, sniff two bottles of smelling
salts dry and must lie down, miss the hangings and have
the Duchess fan her (the poor lady is tyrannised, 'tis a
scandal – and blackmail is rumoured) so that we hear
nothing but the maid's complaints all the way back, when
the rest of the company (in the natural circle of friendship)
wish to discuss the drop and each give his version of the last
confession, in one of which he will protest he is as innocent
as the unborn lamb and in another claim to have been a

highwayman from the age of ten. No sir I will not take ye in the coach for the journey there will be so like the journey to hell ye'd change places with Bob sooner than enter it for the journey back.

MESSENGER (*putting the cup on the table*). No matter sir. My commission demands that I –

ARE. Yet my conscience fears ye will not get through the mob.

MESSENGER. As to that sir, I'll shout 'Clear in the King's name'!

ARE. Never do that! Nay if ye shout that I cannot let ye through the door.

MESSENGER. Is the king not honoured here sir?

ARE. They will suspect ye bring a pardon and pull ye from your horse. 'Twould spoil their day. They have travelled the country since dawn, bought their pennorth of pies and tuppence of beer and practised their song sheets. When a man's hanged the rest of the day's theirs, for riot or sober reflection. When he is not, they work.

MESSENGER. I'm grateful for the warning sir. I'll ride hard with my mouth shut. Now my commission must –

ARE. Wait! (*Aside*.) Must I kill another before breakfast in this room? I shall run out of Bobs.

MESSENGER. Good day sir –

ARE. I have it! I have it! It would go hard with thee to fail in thy commission – I would not see thee and thine suffer it. I cannot take you in my coach – but I may take the pardon.

MESSENGER. But sir my commission says –

ARE. Sir you surprise me! Thou hast dawdled long enough. More delay and I must complain to thy officer. Here are thirty guineas in gold. The bringer of good news is rewarded.

MESSENGER. Thirty guineas!

ARE. 'Tis naught. Fly to the tavern and drink my health. 'Tis a commission. God bless thee. I must dress and jump about.

MESSENGER. I thank your lordship.

The MESSENGER *gives* ARE *the pardon and goes.*

ARE. Now sure I am looked on by a guardian angel – though from whence I know not! I hold in my hand his pardon. I shall not deliver it. What, no lightning stroke? No thunder? The sun does not stop in its course! Lookee Are: thou art a strange soul. I begin to like thee, and I might worship thee. Ye have talents, nay powers I knew not of! Why d'ye live in poverty and marry an ash-raker's daughter? Ye neglect the proper care of thyself. Why have ye not twenty houses? An army? A hundred women? Ye fear Lord this and fawn on Lady that, ye hack your way down the street with your cane – when ye might be carried along it on the backs of the mob! All shall change. There shall be a new world. (*Calls.*) Hedges! Lay out my blue coat and yellow hat. Nay, my pink with the purple plumes. Let us not add to Bob's woes: he shall see a good hat at his hanging. Faith 'tis so spectacular 'twill take his mind off the rope. I shall doff it to the hangman – but Bob may take it as a courtesy to himself. Let the Great Boob hang to prove the world's in its senses. Besides, 'tis heartless to deny a mob. *Noblesse oblige*: Hang him.

Yet I grow fond! Think, I cannot ride up with the pardon! I must forgo the hanging! I take not the coach. I say I go horse-back to go faster. On the way I fall. Racing and hollooing with the joy of glad tidings, over I go tippity-top – knocked out. When I get to my feet the jade hath run. (I shall whip her off. 'Tis a faithful beast and will cling – but I'll break my whip on her, and if that don't serve throw stones.) Then I have my limp. (*Practises.*) Nay severer. (*Practises as he talks.*) I hobble (I have cut a stick from the hedge) to a nearby farm. Deserted. All at the hanging. We have not seen such desolation since the black death. On I crawl. Till time hath run out and poor Bob the Boob is led under the tree. He looks up at heaven – in the direction of the parson's finger – to the welcoming face of god: and all he sees is the black beam above him. I sit in the hedge and weep. Yea, I uncover my head and kneel in the nettles and pray: for the rope to break.

O thou great blazing sun! Great fire of ever-lasting day! My life! My ministering star! Blaze! Blaze! Blaze! Blaze! Hail great sun! Light of the world that I shall stride in! . . . O my friends –

    MOTHER *comes in.*

MOTHER. Blue an' pink's laid out.
ARE. Hedges. Rest in thy chamber.
MOTHER. Keep busy. Cry for him last night, cry later.
ARE. Mothers know best. Lookee, light a fire against my return. The day might yet be cold. Warm thy old hands at the blaze. Here is a paper to start it. (*He gives her the pardons.*)

    ARE *goes.*

MOTHER. Kind on him. Save me fetch the kindlin'. Official. Pretty crown on top. Cut them out for Christmas decoration. (*Shakes her head.*) Best do what yoo're towd. Bob was learnin' to read. (*Tears the papers.*) Ont start that doo yoo ont git the work out the way.

    MOTHER *starts the fire.*

ARE (*off*). Hedges!
MOTHER (*sighing to herself as she stoops – she has become much older*). Now what?

ARE *comes in shouting.*

ARE. 'Tis too much! Hedges will ye make me a fool! Dress me in motley? Set me up as a clown?

MOTHER (*calm, flat*). Sir whatever is the –

ARE. Damned impertinence! Can a man trust nothing! I kept your man when I might have celebrated my title by sacking him! Are you as blind as he?

MOTHER (*calm, flat*). Now sir I'm sure there's no call to –

ARE. No ye did it on purpose! Petty revenge! (*Holds out his blue coat.*) Where is the button! D'ye see it? No! 'Tis off! (*Throws his blue coat on the floor.*) Here, here (*Thumps his chest.*) where every fool can see it! You ancient hag must I sew it myself? I give ye the roof over your head, the ground under your feet, the food on your plate – for a gaping hole with two black spots and a white thread like the lower-anatomy of a mouse! An idiot's badge!

MOTHER. Give it here, I'll see to –

ARE. Now? When it lies in the filth? (*The floor must be filthy since I have not swept it today.*) I must dress like a tramp! O she will sew the button now the coat can't be worn! (*Kicks the coat.*) Madam sew it on and throw the coat in the kennels for my bitch to whelp on. Let her at least have the respect of a full set of buttons. (*Suddenly becomes his old self again.*) Now I must wear my green. So I cannot wear my pink. Twould look like a maypole. I must wear my yellow – which I wore twice at the races. (*Aside.*) 'Tis true I can't go to the hanging. But now the whole county will say 'twas because I could not afford a new hat!

ARE *goes.* MOTHER *mutters to herself as she goes back to the fire.*

MOTHER. Can't sew it on. Ont give me the button.

Suddenly (BOB)

It came suddenly like a bomb
They didn't die with the gestures of dying
They didn't cover their heads in fear
They didn't lift their hands in supplication
They died with the gestures of living

It came suddenly like a bomb
Mouths were open but the words were not spoken
The salt was lifted but wasn't shaken
They died with the gestures of living
Fingers beckoned and hands stretched out to feel
Heads leaned forward in concentration
On words they would never hear

So sudden was the disaster
So swift the moment of fate
It fell at the time of the midday meal
When the fork was halfway between
The mouth and the plate

Scene Eleven

Peterborough.
Holme Cottage. Kitchen. A beer barrel.
MRS WILSON *and* BOB.
BOB *is in shirt sleeves and without fetters. He drinks at the table.*

BOB. When woman? (MRS WILSON *fills his glass. He grabs her arm.*) She's a sly one.
WILSON. Behave or I'll tell Mr Wilson.
BOB (*lets her arm go*). His nibs is quiet. He'll hev to come down for my pardon.

WILSON. Let him sleep. I pulled his door to so he shan't be disturbed.

BOB (*shouts at the ceiling*). Who's in the land of nod? Shh!

WILSON. I'll confiscate your glass.

BOB. Phew. Had enough. Powerful stuff.

WILSON. On your feet. Put your jacket on. Sit there in your shirt sleeves.

BOB (*stands, staggers slightly, steadies himself with one hand on the table*). Oops.

WILSON (*buttons*). Fasten you in.

BOB. Us'll shake hands. Thankyoo sir. Hope yoo hev the same one day. (*Giggles.*) Think when they see how posh I am they most likely give me two pardons.

WILSON. I'll top you up.

BOB (*flat palm over the glass*). Nope. Ont drink 'n'more.

PARSON *and* ROSE *come in*.

Rose! My gal. How I hev miss you. (*Kiss.*) There – thass better now. All's turn out well. The terrible times are over. (*Whispers to* ROSE.) Mrs Wilson say it's come today. Sh! – Parson yoo let your faith wobble but yoo'll git a surprise. Mrs Wilson do the man the honours an' pour his drink. (*Wipes the glass clean on his sleeve.*) Drat spoil me coat. (*Hands the glass to* MRS WILSON.) The letters swim in my head like thass a shipwreck.

PARSON (*low*). Mrs Wilson a drink for his spirits is one thing. But to do this at such an hour is cruel. Wrong. A needless adding to his burdens.

WILSON. I don't need a sermon on how to run a gaol. The profit I make on this it's not worth buying in. (*Gives him the glass.*) No doubt you'll take your glass parson?

PARSON (*slight embarrassment*). Yes yes, thank you. His and my way go differently today.

> MRS WILSON *keeps a tally of the beer that is drunk. She marks it on a slate with chalk.*

BOB. Rose is ought wrong? (*She has her back to him. He turns her. Her face is showered in tears. He steps back. A moment's bewildered fear.*) That . . . ont tears of joy . . . (*Vaguely.*) Why'm I wearin' my best jacket? My pardon come today . . .

PARSON (*hands him an open prayer book*). Read your prayers to me.

BOB. Ont want a lesson!

WILSON (*to* ROSE). Hand me his glass.

BOB. Ay! Less drink! Sorry parson. Why's this gloom fall all around? Rose, ont make my heart sick to see yoo cry. Rose I only lent his lordship my name.

> The PARSON *has three prayer-books open at The Burial of the Dead. He reads and recites Psalm 39 continuously (interrupting himself only once) and the rest of the scene goes on round him. He finally stops reading when he says 'At last. Better. He comes to thee'. After that he prays silently. As the* PARSON *reads from his own book he offers* BOB *the second book open at the place.* BOB *snatches this and throws it on the ground.*

Ont pray at me! Ont be hanged!

> The PARSON *picks up the book while he reads his own.*

Drunk! (*Empties his drink on the floor but does not throw the mug.*)

WILSON. O I see we're going to have one of those days. — He should have been told properly. Not decent treating him like this. — Bobby sit down. Crying won't help.

BOB (*stares at* MRS WILSON). Woman what yoo done? . . . Yoo towd me my pardon was . . . (*Sudden idea.*) Ah!

BOB lurches out. MRS WILSON goes on her knees and mops up the beer.

WILSON. Mrs Hedges stand by him or go outside.
ROSE. He's innocent.
WILSON. They all are if you listen long enough.

Crash upstairs.

There goes the door. That'll cost someone. All this fuss! You come here and behave as if I had nothing better to do.

Crash upstairs.

WILSON (*shouting up*). You wicked boy! (*To the others.*) It's my husband's job. He'll expect his dinner when he gets home. I wish you'd stop cluttering up my kitchen.
BOB (*off*). Ah!
WILSON. There'll be the dickens to pay.
BOB (*off*). Bed made. Cold.

GAOLER comes in with FRANK.
FRANK is drunk.

GAOLER. Cart's outside ma'am. Jist git the horse in.
FRANK (*morose, almost inaudible*).
Old Samson had a daughter, her name was Isabelle
The lily of the valley and the primrose of the dell

When she went a-walking she choosed me for her guide
Down by the Arun river to watch the fishes glide
FRANK (*Sees BOB through the door*). Two of Bob. Have to hang twice.

BOB comes in.

BOB. So I'm to hang. Skinned alive. Rose what'll us do? (*Tries to think. Turns to PARSON.*) Howd his row or I crack his head! (*PARSON prays uninterruptedly.*)

GAOLER. Goo quiet or goo shackled, you hev the choice. (*Pours drinks and raises glass.*) Drink to both gents. Wish I could drink to better times. (*Drinks.*)

BOB. Curses! That a man dies so! Git Are here! That black-guard! Why doo he doo this? When was I angry at him? When did I raise my fist? Touch cap – work quiet – bow – ont that enough? Now he want my head!

FRANK.
The first three months were scarcely o'er,
The young gal lost her bloom
The red fell from her bonny cheeks
And her eyes began to swoon

PARSON (*to* BOB). O do not deny yourself the comfort of his word.

BOB. Yes Frank sing! Kiss me Rose! Yoo ont ashamed of me. How I doo love thee! Ont miss the world: miss thee. (*Jumps onto the table. Poses like the hero of a penny dreadful print.*) Shall we hang? Then hang so high! (*Points up.* FRANK *tries to climb onto the table with him.*)

BOB *and* FRANK.
The next nine months was passed and gone
She brought forth to me a son
And I was quickly sent for
To see what could be done
FRANK (*continues alone*).
I said I should marry her
But o! that would not be
PARSON (*tapping* FRANK *on the back*). My friend open your heart –
FRANK. Git off me yer sinful old bugger! I'll open you!

FRANK *snatches the prayer-books and throws them away.*

The GAOLER *moves in. The* PARSON *motions him back. He closes his eyes and goes on reciting the prayers aloud by heart.* BOB *notices nothing of this but comes down from the table.*

WILSON (*pouring beer*). Four. I keep count so no one's over-charged. (*To* ROSE.) They're allowed one in the cart. I'd offer, but now there's the door to pay . . . (*Pours drinks for everyone.*)

Drum Song (BOB)

A drummer beat upon a drum
And no sound came
He hit the skin
He struck the skin
And no sound came
Wild in his frenzy
A madman sweating blood
He beat he struck he hammered blows
And no sound came
He thrashed and lashed
All through the night
And on into the light
Till his hands bled
Till his eyes bled
Till blood ran from his ears
Till the teeth shook in his head
Till the bones rattled in his body like dice
And still he made no sound
He struck with sticks of iron
With sticks of bone
With sticks of steel
He staggered
He began to reel
In pain

He hammered on
Again! Again!
He crawled upon the ground
He flailed the drum lashed to his side
And no sound came
From the beaten hide
He did not stop till he was dead
    And other men are silent
    When they labour them
    About the head

BOB. The pardon'll come on the square. I can't be so lied to. Rose I'm scared to die. (*Holds her.*)

PARSON. At last. Better. He comes to thee. (*Kneels and prays silently.*)

FRANK. God rot yer Bobby Hedges! I'll pay to go second an' see yer swing. There's justice in this! Yer dragged me to the gallows, yer rantin' hypocrite! Remember the mornin'? If I'd gone with the knife an' fork an' spoon I wouldn't have took the rest! Twelve knives. Ten spoons. Eighteen forks. I'd have been careful then. No drinkin' an' whorin'. Made me way to London like a sane man. Gone round a corner for ever. Safe. Home. The rope don't stretch that far. I hope yer hanging's a cruel one. Yer live to cry mercy on the rope an' don't get it!

    He falls down.

GAOLER (*calling to outside*). She playin' yoo up?

ROSE. Drink. (*Gets glass.*) Bobby.

    BOB *takes the glass and gulps it down.* MRS WILSON *refills* BOB'*s glass and holds him as* ROSE *pours it into his mouth.*

PARSON. Mrs Wilson I'll lodge a complaint.

    GAOLER *picks* FRANK *up and lays him over the barrel.*

ROSE (*tilts* BOB's *head back and pours drink down his throat*).
Drink. Drink. Drink.

PARSON. No! Let him feel the pain or god's anger is not
slaked!

WILSON (*to* BOB). Mr Wilson will help you. You were kind
to him. He won't hurt you. It doesn't take long.

GAOLER (*calling to the outside*). Ready?

BOB (*pushing the glass away*). No. Ont. Clear head. Speak. In
square. Innocent. Englishman. Are's murderer. Murder
me. English.

PARSON. Nay! Who can believe a man who speaks so
harshly? I forbid you to name his lordship. Have you no
gratitude?

BOB. Ay? Ay? Gratitude they want? . . . What can I say? . . .
Who'll hear all I can say?

GAOLER. Pay no heed parson. They say all sorts – (*To* BOB.)
and out there no one listen. They'll shortly give yoo cause
to wish yoo'd saved yoor breath.

VOICE (*off*). She's in.

BOB (*shakes his head to clear it. Then, aside to audience*). I ont
believe this.

> GAOLER *takes* BOB *and* FRANK *out*. FRANK *sings. The*
> PARSON *picks up the three prayer-books and puts on his*
> *last vestments as he follows the others out.*

WILSON (*to* ROSE). You can lie down upstairs. Bed's made.
Clear this mess away. Wish Mr Wilson didn't have to go
out today. When he's had a turn he's nervous. The young
man's waiting for something to go wrong. Then he'll step
in. Some of them would push you in the river to get your
job.

> ROSE *has followed the others out.* MRS WILSON *checks the*
> *amount she has sold.*

Scene Twelve

London Bridge.
ROSE.

ROSE. I stand on London Bridge. Bodies float in the sky and sink towards the horizon. Crocodiles drift in the Thames. On the embankment the plane trees rattle their fingers. Men walk the streets with chains hanging from their mouths. Pillars of black smoke rise between the towers and the temples. The stars will come out like scabs on the sky. There is a gentle breeze.

What have I learned? If nothing, then *I* was hanged.

Man is What He Knows (ROSE)

Does the judge say
I send your arms to prison today
But your feet are free
To walk away?

Does the boss buy
The apple core from the market stall
And leave the skin?
He buys it all

Do the troops shoot
To kill your stomach but not your head?
They shoot to kill
You drop down dead

Once Satan roamed the earth to find
Souls that money could buy
Now he comes to steal your mind
He doesn't wait till you die

Man is what he knows – or doesn't know
The empty men reap death and sow
Famine wherever they march
But they do not own the earth
Sooner believe I could strike it a blow
With my fist and miss!

Geese fly over the moon and do not know
   That for a moment they fill the world with
     beauty
    Flakes do not know where they fall in
      the snow
      Wind and rain cannot tell where
        they blow
        But we may know who we
          are and where we go

  I say these things for me and Bob Hedges. There is a gentle
breeze from the city. I cross the bridge and go into the
streets.

End

Notes

1) This is the PARSON's prayer for Scene Eleven:
I said, I will take heed to my ways: that I offend not in my
tongue. I will keep my mouth as it were with a bridle:
while the ungodly is in my sight. I held my tongue, and
spake nothing! I kept silence, yea, even from good words;
but it was pain and grief to me. My heart was hot within
me, and while I was thus musing the fire kindled: and at
last I spake with my tongue; Lord, let me know mine end,
and the number of my days: that I may be certified how
long I have to live. Behold, thou hast made my days as it
were a span long: and mine age is even as nothing in

respect of thee; and verily every man living is altogether vanity. For man walketh in a vain shadow, and disquieteth himself in vain: he heapeth up riches, and cannot tell who shall gather them. And now, Lord, what is my hope: truly my hope is even in thee. Deliver me from all mine offences: and make me not a rebuke unto the foolish. I became dumb, and opened not my mouth: for it was thy doing. Take thy plague away from me: I am even consumed by means of the heavy hand. When thou with rebukes dost chasten man for sin, thou makest his beauty to consume away, like as it were a moth fretting a garment: every man therefore is but vanity. Hear my prayer, O Lord, and with thine ears consider my calling: hold not thy peace at my tears. For I am a stranger with thee: and a sojourner, as all my fathers were. O spare me a little, that I may recover my strength: before I go hence, and be no more seen. Glory be to the Father, and to the Son: and to the Holy Ghost; as it was in the beginning, is now, and ever shall be: world without end. Amen.

2) Songs.
In the play's first production 'Hurrah' was cut from Scene Eight. In the Royal Shakespeare Company's production in 1988 'Legend of Good Fortune' was cut from Scene Seven. In its place Mrs Hedges sang 'Falkland Song'. The text of this song is printed on page 283.
'Dream Song' could be taken from its place in Scene Eleven and sung between Scenes Ten and Eleven. 'Suddenly' would then have to be cut.
The music for Frank's song in Scene Eleven is the traditional 'Bogie's Bonnie Belle'.

3) An alternative, shorter version of Scene Seven is printed beginning on page 279. If it is used Gabriel does not appear in the play.

4) Comments on directing and acting the play, and especially on Scene eleven, are given in 'Commentary on the War Plays' in *The War Plays* (Methuen Drama, 1991).

Alternative version of Part Two, Scene Seven:

Part Two

[Scene Seven]

Hilgay.
The Hall.
Workroom.
MRS HEDGES *peels potatoes.* ROSE *comes in.*

ROSE. They found 'im guilty.

MOTHER (*continues to peel potatoes*). Only t'be anticipated.
  'Is lordship'll take care of it.

ROSE. Are killed 'er. Bob's coverin' up.

MOTHER (*stops peeling in alarm*). Howd yoor row, gal.
  Yoo'll git us all threw out on us necks. I know what
  you're up to. Hardache's come. Waitin' outside. Say
  yoo wrote 'im. Yoo let on what's gooin' on 'ere, I'll
  cuss the day you wed my Bob.

ROSE. Hardache'll 'elp 'im.

MOTHER. Ont need help.

ROSE. They'll 'ang 'im.

MOTHER. Ont talk so far back! No sense of proportion.
  This is 'is big chance. Doo 'is lordship a favour like this
  'e's set up for life. (*Starts peeling potatoes again.*) Poor
  people can't afford t' waste a chance like this. God know
  it ont come often. Time our luck change. Yoo start
  trouble, 'oo pay? Us. *Yoo're* back t'London, *we* git
  chuck out. End up in the work'ouse: work like a slave,
  work'ouse disease – ont last six month. See it afore. Too
  old t' 'ave my life mess up. So ont meddle, Rose.

ROSE. Bob's in prison waitin' t' be –

MOTHER. Worse places outside. Ont expect 'is lordship t'goo in the dock for the like of 'er. Jist drag the family name through the mire. Whatever next! Ont know where t'look next time I goo t' the village, they know I work for someone like that. 'S'n accident *who* it was. Silly woman deserved t'git killed. She come into my kitchen dress up, I give 'er a whack a my fryin' pan she ont git up from.

ROSE. 'E's 'anged but the roof's over your 'ead.

MOTHER. Yoo think I'm that sort of a woman, my dear, thass yoor privilege.

ROSE. I don't understand you people! Why should Arse-face 'elp 'im? Bob's a labourer, no better than a –

MOTHER. Jist ont stand in my boy's way when 'e hev 'is chance t'goo up in the world. Lie on oath doo it 'elp 'im, say I saw 'im stick the sword in her gut. 'Sides, even if what yoo say's true – which it ont – if my Bob stood up in court an' spoke *rashness* 'bout 'is lordship, 'ood believe 'im? Ont yoo know nothin', gal? If there's a row between man an' boss, stand t'reason 'oo win.

ROSE. It ain' between man and boss. It's between two bosses.

MOTHER (*still peeling potatoes*). Now whass she on about?

ROSE. It pays t'know the law when you're black. You're not allowed t'benefit from your own crime. (MOTHER *snorts in derision.*) If Are killed 'is wife, 'e loses 'er money. (MOTHER *stops peeling.*) It goes back to the next of kin: 'er father.

> HARDACHE *steps in. He carries a walking stick and with his hat fans his face, neck and inside his jacket.*

HARDACHE (*gesturing behind him*). Pretty place. (*To* ROSE.) Saw you crossin' the fields so I followed you in. Sorry I missed the funeral. Carry on, Mrs – Hedges in't it? (MOTHER *starts to peel potatoes again.*) A neighbour had to sell up and I couldn't miss the opportunity. Then the trial: I had to arrange a little shares shenanigans. Rose, you married a villain but no one's perfect. All the bitterness was squeezed out of me long ago when my first warehouse went up on fire. Tell Bob I haven't wept since.

MOTHER (*stops peeling potatoes*). That wicked gal's got it in 'er 'ead my Bob ont do it.

HARDACHE. Not do it? Is that right, Rose? Then who did?

ROSE. Are.

HARDACHE. His lordship? Nay, I've never 'eard the like. Happy young couple like that? Why ever should he be so rash? No no, she were struck down by your over-hasty young man. I can't believe otherwise – his lordship, you say?

MOTHER (*peeling*). Yoo talk sense into 'er, sir.

HARDACHE. Well, I'm struck both ways sideways. (MOTHER *goes on peeling but watches* HARDACHE *intently*.) What a predicament to fall into our laps – (*Quickly correcting himself.*) land on our heads. A real taremadiddle and no mistake. Did he strike her, Rose?

ROSE. Yes sir and talked Bob into taking the blame.

HARDACHE. I shan't take kindly to bein' deceived, Mrs Hedges. Now's the time to speak out. You know what's at stake: my daughter's memory. D'you know owt?

MOTHER (*carefully peeling*). Well – I doo an' I don't. What should I say?

HARDACHE. The truth woman! It's a Christian country in't it?

MOTHER (*as before*). Well – if 'is lordship kill 'er – what's the good of what I say?

HARDACHE. What good? Does justice count for nothin' in these parts? When I think of that innocent young man – you did say he was innocent, Rose? – alone in his cell,

my withers weren't more wrung for me own daughter.
Well Mrs Hedges?

MOTHER. I suppose – if that's 'ow it is – (*She stops peeling.*)
I hev t'tell Mr Hardache my son towd me 'e ont do it.

HARDACHE. And also testified Are cajoled him into
covering up his own crime. What a dastardly villain!

MOTHER (*finishing repeating his words in her attempt to
memorize them. The peeling knife and a potato are held up in
the air over the bowl*). . . . coverin' up 'is own crimes
what a dastardly villain.

HARDACHE. Well. Now we know. I'm right glad I came
to pay respects to my daughter's grave: you run into
business anywhere. (*To* ROSE.) Leave all to me lass.
Mind, no speakin' out of turn. The fish still has to be
landed by an expert tickler. Good day.

ROSE. Will you go straight to the judge?

HARDACHE. Tch, tch, didn't I say leave all to me?

ROSE. I'll show you the stairs to the –

HARDACHE. Nay, I can't be seen ascendin' from the
servants' quarters. Best slip out the way I came and go
round to the front. Don't want to put suspicion into his
lordship's mind if 'e's acquired the habit of murder.
(HARDACHE *goes out the way he came.*)

MOTHER. Ont stand there, gal! Take these out an' git 'em
on the stove. Dinner'll come 'round t'day jist as it did
yesterday. (ROSE *goes out with the bowl of peeled potatoes.*)

This song can be sung in Scene Seven in place of 'Legend of Good Fortune'.

Falkland Song (MOTHER)

My son why have you broken my leg?
My son why have you crushed my arm?
My son why did you tear the hair from my head?
My son when did I do you any harm?
My son you don't hear what I say

You lie in a hole with your broken leg
Your arms are crushed and hold emptiness
Your skinhead is cracked like a helmet of steel
You're dead and you don't feel any pain
My son you don't hear what I say

My leg is broken – my arms are crushed
My breast was torn by the bayonet thrust
I bear all the pains a soldier bore
But you're dead and you don't feel your pain anymore
And you don't hear what I say

I don't know what the Spanish for suffering is
Or the Spanish for mother or son or war
Or the Spanish for winter or summer or pain
Or for waste or for wounds or for wind or for rain

My son it isn't for you that I mourn
And I don't feel the pain of your flesh being torn
I weep for the enemy you shot at Bluff Bay
When the sun stood high on a cold winter day
For the enemy you butchered on Tumbledown Height
In the bayonet charge of the army of night
But you don't hear what I say

What is the Spanish for gun and for bomb?
What is the Spanish for SAS and hell?

What is the Spanish for night?
What is the Spanish for innocence?
What is the Spanish for fight?
What is the Spanish for hooligan?
What is the Spanish for pain?
What is the Spanish for government?
What is the Spanish for wind and for cold and for rain?

My son they told you you died for me
You killed to set your countrymen free
But I mourn for the soldier you killed by the sea
I curse you with each blast of wind from the shore

You sleep in peace – don't feel pain anymore
I curse you with the shout of each breaking wave
You murdered your brother – you murdered your brother
For he was my son – he was my son
Though he spoke only Spanish and never knew me
You murdered my son by the cold winter sea
For I was his mother – I was his mother
And you made my womb a grave

What is Spanish for money?
What is Spanish for shares?
What is Spanish for he is the loser who dares?
What is Spanish for loss?
What is Spanish for gain?
What is Spanish for dividends?
What is Spanish for pain?
What is Spanish for wind and for cold and for rain?
My son you are dead and I ask in vain

Restoration

The music

Given here are the melodies composed by Nick Bicât for the play. Full orchestration can be obtained from London Management & Representation Ltd, 235 Regent Street, London W1R 7AG.

ROSES (BOB)

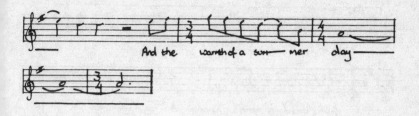

And the warmth of a sum — mer day —

SONG OF LEARNING (FRANK)

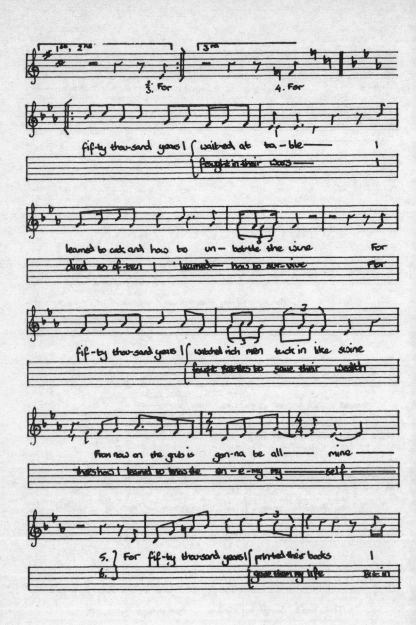

3. For

4. For

fif-ty thou-sand years I ∫ waited at ta-ble——

⟨ fought in their wars——

learned to cook and how to un-bottle the wine

died as often I ⟨ learned— how to sur-vive

For

For

fif-ty thou-sand years I ∫ watched rich men tuck in like swine

⟨ fought battles to save their wealth

From now on the grub is gon-na be all—— mine ——

that's how I learned to know the en-e-my my —— self

5. ⟩ For fif-ty thou-sand years I ∫ printed their books

6. ⟨ ⟨ gave them my life   But in

learned to read by looking over their shoulder   For
all that time they never learned how to live —   For

fif-ty thou-sand years I { built li-braries for men of   wealth —
      { was go-verned by men of   wealth —

That's how I learned to write the books I need my-self ————
Now I have learned to make the laws up for my-self ————

I have known pain and bowed be-fore beau-ty shared in joy and died —

— in du-ty   Fif-ty thou-sand years I lived with ————   I

learned how to blow up your   hell.

DREAM (ROSE)

THE WOOD SONG (MOTHER)

The wooden cra-dle — the wooden spoon the wooden ta-ble — The wooden
bed — The wooden house the wooden beam The wooden pit-jit the wooden
bench The wood-en ham-mer the wood-en stair The wood-en gallows the wooden
box The iron chain the brace-lets the hu-man toil — the earthly span —
These are the lot of eve-ry man — The winds that drive the somewhat blast for
eve-ry man the die is cast All you — who would re-sist your fate strike

8. keyboard plays solo from
8. until faded.

SONG OF THE CALF (BOB)

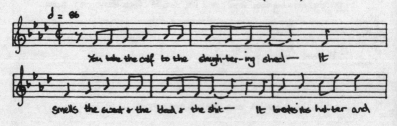

You take the calf to the daugh-ter-ing shed — It
smells the sweat & the blood & the shit — It beats its hot-ter and

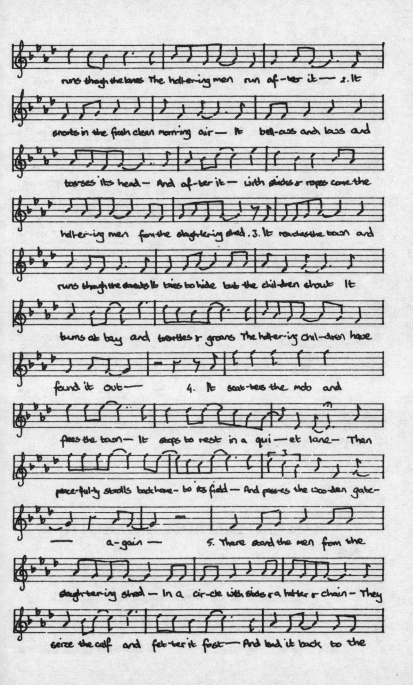

runs through the lanes The haltering men run af-ter it — 2. It

snorts in the fresh clean morning air — It bel-ows and laws and

tosses its head — And af-ter it — with sticks or ropes come the

halter-ing men from the slaughtering shed. 3. It reaches the town and

runs through the streets It tries to hide but the chil-dren shout It

turns at bay and trembles & groans The halter-ing chil-dren have

found it out — 4. It scat-ters the mob and

flees the town — It stops to rest in a qui — et lane — Then

peace-ful-ly strolls back home — to its field — And passes the woo-den gate —

— a-gain — 5. There stand the men from the

slaughtering shed — In a cir-cle with sticks or a halter & chain — They

seize the calf and fet-ter it fast — And lead it back to the

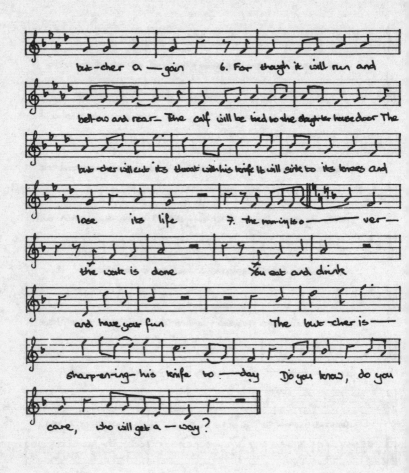

but-cher a-gain 6. For though it will run and

bell-ow and rear— The calf will be tied to the slaughter house door The

but-cher will cut its throat with his knife It will sink to its knees and

lose its life 7. The roaming is o——ver—

the work is done You eat and drink

and have your fun The but-cher is—

sharp-en-ing his knife to—day Do you know, do you

care, who will get a——way?

A MAN GROANS (ROSE AND MOTHER)

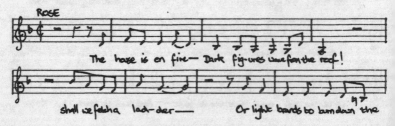

ROSE

The house is on fire— Dark fig-ures wave from the roof!

shall we fetch a lad-der—— Or light bands to burn down the

THE GENTLEMAN (BOB AND ROSE)

who would raise their voice when soft words will do— my friend?

Why use a knife— when a smile makes— cuts that

bleed?— when you have the mind— why—

both-er to chop off the head? When white hands will—

— do the work why make your hands— red—

SONG OF TALKING (FRANK AND BOB)

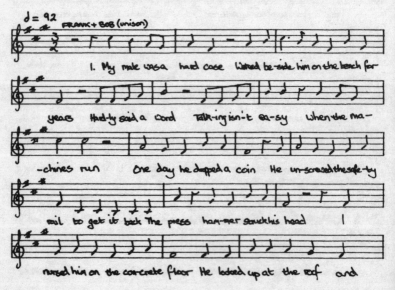

♩ = 92

FRANK + BOB (unison)

1. My mate was a hard case Worked be-side him on the beach for

years Hard-ly said a word Talk-ing isn't ea-sy when the ma-

-chines run One day he dropped a coin He un-screwed the safe-ty

rail to get it back The press ham-mer squashed his head

nursed him on the concrete floor He looked up at the roof and

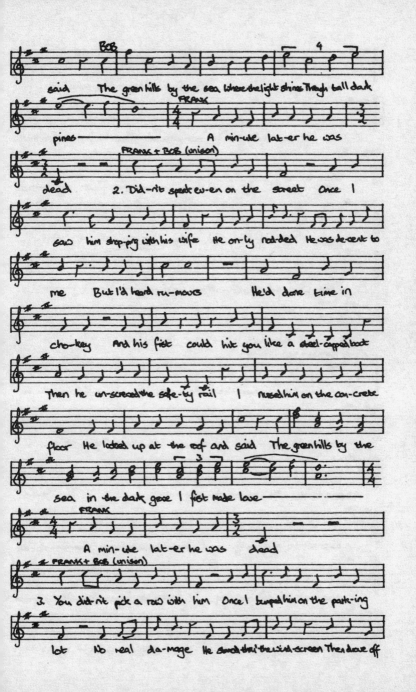

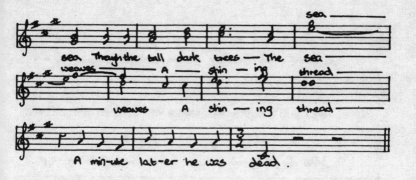

sea Though the tall dark trees — The sea

weaves A shin-ing thread

weaves A shin-ing thread

A min-ute lat-er he was dead.

LEGEND OF GOOD FORTUNE (MOTHER)

Men lived in peace and plen-ty When the world was as young as the

day But a god came down from heav-en And

took the good things a-way He put them all in a

bas-ket And slow-ly climbed up to his cave He

put the bas-ket un-der his head and slept like a wea-ry

slave There — passed on earth ten

a-ges of war Men groaned and lived as the dead then this

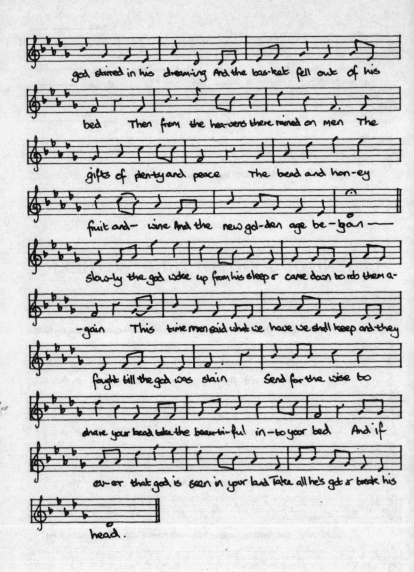

god stirred in his dreaming And the bas-ket fell out of his
bed   Then from the hea-vens there rained on men   The
gifts of plen-ty and peace   The bead and hon-ey
fruit and— wine And the new gol-den age be—gan—
slow-ly the god woke up from his sleep & came down to rob them a-
-gain   This time men said what we have we shall keep and they
fought till the god was slain   Send for the wise to
share your bead take the beau-ti-ful in—to your bed   And if
ev-er that god is seen in your land Take all he's got & break his
head.

SONG OF THE CONJUROR (ROSE AND BOB)

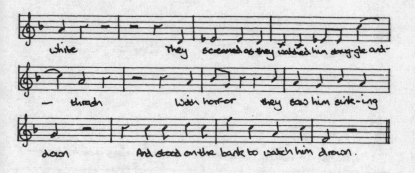

white They screamed as they watched him struggle and—

— thrash With horror they saw him sink-ing

down And stood on the bank to watch him drown.

TREE OF LIBERTY (ROSE AND FRANK)

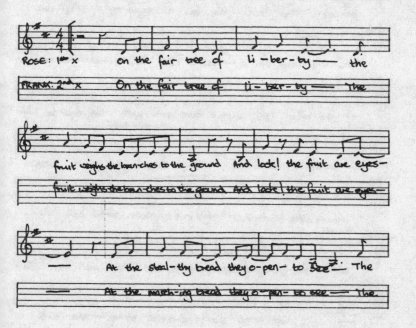

ROSE: 1st x on the fair tree of li-ber-ty— the

FRANK: 2nd x On the fair tree of li-ber-ty— The

fruit weighs the bran-ches to the ground And look! the fruit are eyes—

fruit weighs the bran-ches to the ground And look! the fruit are eyes—

— At the steal-thy bread they o-pen— to see— The

— At the march-ing bread they o-pen— to see— The

strike like thun—der bolts the rest are re-freshed in its cool

— green— shade

And

so the fair tree grows— As tall as the pine and as strong

FRANK + ROSE

— as the oak— Wreathed with the wild rose— & the hanging vine

— As our fore-fa-thers spoke and so the fair tree grows-

As tall as the pine and as strong—

— as the oak— Wreathed with the wild rose r the hanging vine

— As our fore-fa-thers spoke.

SUDDENLY (BOB)

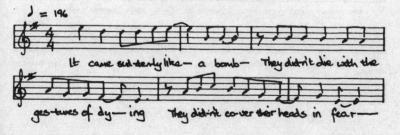

♩ = 196

It came suddenly like— a bomb— They didn't die with the

ges-tures of dy—ing They didn't cover their heads in fear—

THE DRUM SONG (BOB)

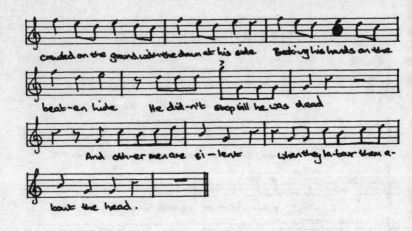

crawled on the ground with the down at his side Beating his hands on the

beat-en hide   He did-n't stop till he was dead

And oth-er men are si — lent   When they la-bour them a-

bout the head.

MAN IS WHAT HE KNOWS (ROSE)

Does the judge say I send your arms to prison to-day But your

feet are free— To walk a-way? Does the boss buy the a-pple

core from the market stall and   leave the skin?   He

buys it all— Do the troops shoot to kill your stomach but not your head?

shoot to kill— You drop down dead Once   Sa-tan roamed the earth

— to find— souls that he could buy—No one cares to steal

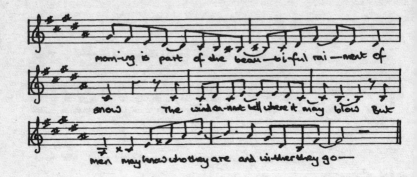

Restoration

Poems and Stories

Poets

On the radio the poets said
Poets should not speak of happiness but joy
As if on the floor of the salt ocean
There rose a spring of pure water
And death tasted better to those who drowned
Once to explain evil to a seminarist
I told him of the guard who helped old people
Into the gas chamber as gently as if
He helped his mother to cross the street
The seminarist said christ is in everyone
And took joy in his god who visited death camps
Since then I have avoided seminarists
Prisoners praise the sun at cell windows
The poor hop like sparrows over crumbs
And slaves clean their chains in love of brightness
Joy lives with pain and so outlasts happiness
And evil is its own reward
The evil act out of love and goodness of heart
The state of evil is terrible: it is joyful
The guard will die for the fatherland with the joy
That makes him bear the misery of service
If poets would be joyful
Let them eat with the hungry and work with the slaves
But because when they write they must be free
It is the job of poets to build prisons

A Hand

A man passed his neighbour's house. Through the window he saw something on the table. He wanted it.

That evening he sat at home after his meal and watched television. Suddenly the thing came into his head. He thought about it for a minute. Then he shook himself and concentrated on television. Next morning he woke with the thing in his head. He thought about it on and off through the day. As he came home in the evening he looked in his neighbour's window. The thing was still on the table. He stopped. Suddenly the curtain was jerked to across the window. He saw his neighbour's fingers clutching the edge of the curtain as he jerked it. Once or twice he had quarrelled with his neighbour.

Next day the man thought he might offer to buy the thing. But he knew his neighbour would not sell it for what he had to offer.

That night the man could not sleep. He thought of ways to get the thing. His neighbour was usually at home. He would wait till he went out. Then he would break in at the back of the house. He would walk through to the kitchen and . . . but the thing wouldn't be on the table. His neighbour would have hidden it. He had seen him looking at it. The man was just about to scratch the back of his neck when he felt a large hand placed on his head. He started and turned round to see who had stolen into his room. His work supervisor? His neighbour? There was no one.

But a moment ago a hand had touched his head. As a threat? Or was it a pat? He couldn't be sure because his startled movement had pushed the hand away. Deeply perplexed he was just going to scratch his brow – as his hand reached the level of his eyes he saw it had grown. It was half as large again as its normal size. He turned it over. The knuckles were white and knotted. The nails made him think of the doors of dollshouses. It was his own hand he'd felt on his head.

He must go to the doctor in the morning. When he woke the thing was in his head. The hand had grown. He was afraid to go to the doctor. He would send him to a specialist hospital – an institute for freaks. By mid-day his hand was four times its natural size. He didn't feel shocked. He felt numb. It might have been someone else's hand growing.

In the afternoon he dozed off in exhaustion. He dreamed of the thing. He woke with the idea in his head that the hand was growing to help him. It must be so. It was already five or six times its proper size. He wouldn't have to go into his neighbour's house. He would reach in from outside. Open doors, rummage in cupboards, turn out drawers. He trusted his hand. He stared with respect at the great strange shape. It was as cumbersome as a bull's carcass. The lifeline was as deep as a ditch. The fingerprints were like furrows on a forehead. Why should he be afraid? When he'd got the thing the hand would shrink. There wouldn't be any need for it to be big. Of course he couldn't explain *everything* – but only the ignorant thought you had to do that. He kissed the hand.

By now it was so big he couldn't tell how quickly it was growing. He couldn't hold a tape-measure to measure it. Its size made him awkward. It was as if he was one-handed. He fed and dressed himself with his other hand. He carried the big hand round as a dead weight. Sometimes he forgot – he tried to use it and broke things. He looked forward to the day when the hand would stop growing. Then he would know it was time to ransack his neighbour's house. After all, it would be silly to come away with just one thing when his hand was making such an effort to help him.

Next morning he didn't wake up. The heaviness of his hand had tired him. He slept for three days. This was a pity. When he woke the hand was bigger than the rest of his body.

The man felt that at last the time had come to go to his neighbour's house. If his neighbour was in he would hide behind his hand. Or use it to push his neighbour into the yard. No one would believe his crazy story about a giant hand. The man giggled with excitement.

He dressed. He couldn't put on his shirt in the usual way. He put his left arm into the left sleeve. He wrapped the right sleeve round his neck. He crept from his bedroom. He had to be careful to hold the hand up off the ground. But then it blocked his view. It seemed to take him half an hour to reach the bottom of the stairs. He crept along the hall to the front door. Fortunately this was locked with a bolt. He slid the bolt and awkwardly fumbled the door open by squeezing along the edge of it with his hand. He stepped back. He felt cold air from the street. There was a crash. As he'd stepped forward to leave his house his hand had slammed the door in his face. He couldn't find the bolt. Perhaps his hand had knocked it off.

The man was worried. The hand was meant to help him get into his neighbour's house. Now it had made him a prisoner in his own. It began to grow much faster. He turned round in the hall. He would still be able to squeeze himself up the stairs to his bedroom. He wanted to lie down. Then he thought it would be better to get to the kitchen. He tried to push the hand before him. It was like trying to push an elephant. Suddenly he saw it was foolish to try to push it. Instead he used the fingers as legs – as children do when they play hand-puppets.

The great five-legged carcass soon set the rest of him in motion. His feet couldn't reach the ground. He was attached to the hand like a little tail on a pig's rump. As the hand moved he seemed to be wriggling with pleasure.

The hand stuck in the kitchen doorway. With the fingers he tore off the doorposts and made a bigger hole. The hand bundled into the kitchen with a slurping, unblocking sound. The man could still use his will on the fingers. If only the room were bigger he could even enjoy himself! Dance with five legs! He tried to twist the hand round – or make the hand twist him round. He wanted to get to the sink. He wanted to drink some water. He couldn't get to the sink. The hand was pressing him to the wall. If he could get to the kitchen table . . . to the knives in the drawer. He could take out a knife with his other hand. He'd cut himself free. Or stab the hand. There would be a lot of blood but that wouldn't matter.

By now the hand grew so fast he heard the great tendons and muscles creaking and groaning and snapping. His arm and shoulder were being sucked into a wall of flesh. If he could he would have bitten through his wrist but it was buried deep in the flesh.

Even now he could control his fingers – but awkwardly. The kitchen walls were squeezing them in a vice. If he could manoeuvre them he'd tear down the kitchen and prise himself free. Float on this swamp of flesh. Breathe. Make a plan. For the first time for many hours he thought of the thing he'd seen on his neighbour's table. Not angrily or covetously. He just saw it as a mirror might reflect it. It's said that when someone drowns they see their whole life. As his hand engulfed him he saw the thing. He felt he was being trodden down by a voiceless crowd. He seemed to hear their feet. It was the blood pounding in the great hand. His struggles to free himself became the pressure that crushed him. He was squeezed to death by his own fist.

The kitchen walls cracked. The ceiling twisted and rose. The gas main exploded. The house went up in the air. The house next door lost its windows.

Only fragments of the man were found. There seemed to be a lot of them. The ambulance men said it always seemed to be like that.

The Falklands Quotations and Poems

I Press

'Skinhead Ian "Walter" Mitty would put the frighters on anyone. With his close-shaved head, tattoo-covered body and heavy bovver boots, he looks every inch what he is – a hard man. But Walter, 20, from Richmond, Yorkshire, was near to tears yesterday when he learnt that his dearest wish – to get at the Argies with his bare hands – had been denied.' – *Reporter*[1]

Precision technology invented by scientists and built
    by skilled engineers
Was used in the state-of-the-art comms room
On HMS Invincible
To send this report
From the task force
To a newspaper

And later violent denunciations of football louts
Were published by the same press
That complains of the impurity of the water
While it swims in its own cess

II High Opinions

'I have a high opinion of 3 Para; they were very hard men. Some of them said they had only joined because they could kill legally.' – *Falkland Islander*[2]

Only the very wise know what they do
They know they may not ask too much
And that their questions should not lead
To questions of greater ignorance

Not that we should be patient with fools
Or sit with torturers or work for the sellers of lies
But that the mother tongue we speak and hear each day
Is the language which must be translated to us
Before we understand what we say and hear

If anyone has a high opinion of those who wish to kill
We should ask what *they* wished who made the killing
    legal
The orator is responsible for what the mob says
And politicians for crimes their acts make legal
Where torture is legal many have high opinions of those
    hard enough to torture
If gutters could think they'd have high opinions of
    sewage
But gutters keep their innocence: they only seem to
    gurgle with glee as they devour filth

Once conquerors boasted of the numbers they'd killed
After Hiroshima they claimed the number was less
We need not believe every lout's posturings
But the bones of dead patriots murmur and corrupt the
    mother land in which they're buried
It would be better to cast their bones in the gutter and let
    the rain babble harmlessly over them
And when we're told to Rejoice! Just rejoice!
    It would be wiser to shudder

III Titus 9

A newspaper ran a daily competition for 'Argy-Bargie'
jokes. Nine-year-old Titus won £5 for a joke about two
British soldiers killing hundreds of 'Argy' soldiers.[3]

Five pounds for a little boy's story
Of a few hundred Argies dead
What sort of tales do they tell you

As they tuck you into bed?
With luck you'll have a nightmare
Full of bleeding Argie wops
And wake in the night and scream
Then write and tell us how many you saw
And your number might come up tops
In our 'Bingo-War-Game Dream'
If you claim thousands of bodies
And thousands and thousands more
And are careful how you spell
We'll send you a ton of ice cream
For helping our paper win
The Great Circulation War
But Titus 9 of Brighton
Hear this and remember well
The laughter of devils is louder
Than the groans of the damned in hell
And the colour of black-and-white is red
When papers have blood to sell
In the language of Shakespeare say it
While jackals howl in the pit
We should speak and write only that
Which is seemly and decent and fit
For many millions have perished
By bombs and bullets and swords
But beyond all counting are those who were
Sent to their death by words

IV An Armchair

He sat in a heavy armchair
Many summers had faded the cloth and time had become
    its pattern as if it could be bought from a superior
        sales catalogue
His brown shoes were cleaned with three brushes

One dubbed cream – one gave the first polish – one the
    gentleman's finish
Two brushes scraped and flattened his yellow-grey hair
Where his flannels stretched tight over his thighs the
    creases were two rigid lines
His sportsjacket and waistcoat were cut from the same
    check
And there was a tartan tie
With the marks of old knots crushed into the cloth like a
    wizened Lilliputian throat hanging under the knot
When he went into the world he tied his tie in rage
His mouth rarely closed and over it like a wraith of
    smoke from a pit there was a small moustache
His eyes were intense but dead like eyes cut from a
    photograph – upturned bottles askew in a standing
      ocean
His stomach bulged – it might have been cut from an
    animal and awkwardly strapped onto him with a
      truss
In one hand he held a tumbler of gin and tonic and ice
And said
The wisp of smoke moved heavily as if the pit gave off
    swamp gas
And the creases in the tie were as grey as the encrustations
    and scourings left by years of rain under a drain
      spout
And I saw his fingernails were flat as if they'd been
    trodden on
And the ice in his tumbler was still
        We must turf 'em out
        Know our local lads are keen for a crack at 'em
        Die for our liberties like in my young day
In the room there was silence
The armchair aged in the sun
Authority had handed me a form with a box to fill in

He rattled his ice – it clinked like a toy sabre
He was an elderly man – older than the armchair and the
    elm that would coffin him had long been old
The friends of his youth lay at Arnheim and their fathers
    at Flanders
And the horrors I thought I would be spared because so
    many had suffered them
Were there
Time had gone and nothing is learned and no one is
    spared
Cruelty drinks gin from a tumbler and evil talks as if it
    read a cartoon
And we are killed by the horror in the armchair

V Change

'On the way down [to the Falklands], this chap had been
saying that he would never be able to press the button
when the time came; he could never kill someone like that.
Later, after his first Sea Dart firing, someone asked him
how he felt. "Bloody marvellous".'[4]

The weapon has not changed
Your uniform has not changed
The enemy's uniform has not changed
The buttons and buckles and zips ripped open on gaping
    camouflage combat-jackets have not changed
Rain soaks the blood dried into camouflage combat-
    jackets and it runs
Rain and blood do not change
The water through which missiles travel has not changed
The water in dead men's boots does not change
The sky through which missiles travel does not change
The albatross and gull hear men's curses and warning
    cries as they hear one sheep call to another

Their business is land to nest and shore to pillage: they
    scream and are not changed
The earth which is torn open by missiles does not change
Earth corrupts the body and neither is changed
The dead in camouflage combat-jackets seemed dressed in
    crumbled maps of the land they died for and are not
      changed
Give the dead maps and they do not march
Set them up in motley and they do not dance
The soldier falls back from the bayonet and writhes on his
    trench floor like a corpse gnashing its teeth in the
      grave and the worms wake in their clay walls and
      are not changed
It is the same with dust as with sand: unchanging
And it is the same with rock
Fire begets smoke but it drifts away – and if the fire is
    ardent it drives the smoke from it
This lesson is taught on battlefields and in hallways and
    other places
Your children will grow but you will not know it because
    you will not see whether their eyes are changed
When they run to greet you the dead enemy will place his
    hands over their eyes
If they stumble he will catch them and laugh
And when you call to them in anger or loneliness – after
    your kind – he will weep for you
The dead cannot take away their hands
The enemy you killed has not changed
He is merely dead
You are changed
And now you must return to your children and city

VI Ajax Bay

'When the first one went down, right in front of us, straight into the water off Ajax Bay, it seemed as though the whole Commando Brigade stood up and cheered and clapped and jumped for joy.' – *Marine*[5]

The false camaraderie of ranks divided by class
When leaders cannot let down their lads
And the led must respect the officer gentlemen
So that sentimentality corrupts violence
Making it mawkish sustained and bloodier
And the jeering and monkey–dancing as men are killed
      and burned and mutilated
And the officers' brutal efficiency and nabob–clumsiness
And the rank-pique that kills the led
Yet putting all this aside
Men went bare-handed into fires to bring out wounded
And set down helicopters on white cliff-faces shrouded in
      blizzard snow
Certainly there was good here
And we regret that persistence is turned to stubbornness
And great skill into a wizard's tricks
At home many are left to rot in sickness
And many innocent shut in prisons of paper stone panic
      and listless despair.
This waste! – for the lease on a millstone
And a bogland for sheep and geese and graves

VII Crosses

To tighten its grip on power a reactionary government
      invaded the islands
To tighten its grip on power a reactionary government
      invaded the islands that had been invaded

A reactionary government lost
A reactionary government won
A reactionary government fell
A reactionary government tightened its grip on power
A reactionary government stood trial
A reactionary government held elections
A reactionary government was condemned by the people
A reactionary government was re-elected by the people
    The ballot papers could have been marked with
        upright crosses

The Lord of the Beasts

How inefficient is the Lord of the Beasts!
The jaguar brings down the doe in seconds
The fish darts from the rock and quickly devours the
    meal speared on its snout
The hawk hovers but is swift in the drop
If it flies off to nestlings the little mouse gripped in its
    talons as if gift-wrapped by Lucifer is already dead
The cat couldn't fall on its prey faster if it were a pencil
    that drew it
And it doesn't play with it because it can't work out how
    to kill it but to sharpen its skills
It's true snakes engorge a rabbit as slowly as if they
    gave birth to it backwards: but that's not because
        they're condemned forever to choke on the apple
           but because they wolf their food whole like
             Man the Lord of the Beasts!
Man obliterates thousands in a flash (praise where it's due)
    as if they had never been
But the rest?
Some of the gassed took years to die
Children he's attacked – and not with the furtive efforts
    of a lonely street-lurker but assisted by pals and
        encouraged by bonuses and every token of
           honour – linger for days
Some even hang on for years and die at a great age when
    a bug (of which he claims to be lord) brings them
        down in an hour
After a battle he leaves the field littered with wounded
    muttering scorn or bellowing taunts at his
        incompetence
And after an air raid people only half dead skulk under
    the rubble and jeer 'can't catch me!'

The world is full of his failures

Those in the jungle he can ignore – but at home he must
      build houses to hide people so fit they lie on their
         back in bed for years

And many are left to parade the streets and taunt him
      with their crutches and plastic limbs – their
         wheelchairs and faces like joke masks

Out of respect for his feelings you contrive not to see
      them but who could deny them their right to mock?

If the lamb gets away it's because the lion is old or
      dyspeptic

But men go out killing in their prime – and they're not
      restricted to natural weapons like the other poor
         beasts – they have the most modern equipment

And it's his favourite occupation – yet even jackals and
      hyenas could give him some tips!

The Lord of the Beasts is an inefficient killer

You'd think he'd be ashamed to kneel at his thanksgiving
      services

Or is he kneeling in shame at how many got away?

A Story

There was once a rich man
To get rich he did many bad things
He stole a dustbin from an old woman and sold it back to
      her with an anti-theft device
He lent money and made the borrowers repay twice as
      much
He made the poor work for him and took half of what
      they earned so that they paid him to keep them poor
But he didn't mind: he was rich
Only one thing worried him
Down the road lived another rich man
Now our man knew how he'd got his own money and he
      said to himself
This other man must be as wicked as me
So he didn't trust him: he slept with a pistol under his
      head
That should've made him feel safe
But it didn't
Did the pistol still work?
Were the bullets dud?
Perhaps his neighbour could creep like a cat and come
      with his gun to rob him
So he sat up all night trying to keep awake and nodding
      off over his pistol
Sometimes he woke with a start
Sometimes the pistol fell from his hands and he snatched
      at it
Once he saw a shadow creeping towards his bed
He fired
The safety catch was on
After that he tried to stay awake with the safety catch off
You could see him bent over the muzzle

Gaunt and tired
Grizzled stubble on his chin
Nodding and muttering and cursing his neighbour
The man who knew what thieves were because he was a
     thief and who put a pistol under his head so that he
          could sleep in peace
Lived in terror
And one day he nodded off and shot himself

Sports Ground Inferno

Ranks of spectators in the wooden stand

Excitement! Sensation! – the match swings this way and
that

Sudden heat – spectators look round – they watch the
clothes of others near them smoulder and burst into
flames

The floor crackles – in an instant the roof is a rolling sea
of fire

Those who escape to the pitch look back

In the bright furnace they see dark blemishes like lumps
of coal – bodies

A man in blazing clothes and with an expressionless face
comes from the flames

And strolls – that is the word witnesses will use later –
over the pitch

Others sit upright in their seats as flames run between
them along the handrails

They do not seem to know what is happening to them or
what they might do to save themselves

Later that day survivors will stand by the charred corpses
and tell how they had felt they were in a dream

And in this way one Saturday afternoon as women
worked or drank tea with their neighbours and
children played or fed their pets

The little holocaust fell on the busy city where many
dreamed and did not know what they might do to
save themselves

Water

In a certain city there had been for many hundreds of years a shortage of water. This caused disease and other suffering to the citizens. Each spring there was a heavy rainfall and the silent people watched the precious life-stream running in gutters that would soon be as dry as bone. In time modern machines were constructed. There were new spinning factories and iron foundries in the city. These places needed more water and so did the new workers. The city's rulers were practical and philanthropic men. They used their new machines to build a dam in the hills over the city. The dam collected all the water the city needed. Unfortunately when the spring rains fell the lake behind the dam became too full. There was a danger that the pressure of water would explode and engulf the city in sudden destruction. The dam wall shook like the hand of a sick man. This terrified the workers and some of them ran away from the factories and lived in the hills. In the general panic there was rioting and looting. Priests held special services. Factory owners called on the government to enforce law and order.

As the rulers of the city had been clever enough to build the dam they ought to have been clever enough to make it safe. They might have built aqueducts to take the water safely round the city or through the parks and squares to make them beautiful with lakes and fountains. But understand that there was panic and fear of collapse. In such times rulers don't blame the machinery of society but its people. Indeed they look on disaster as a test of national spirit. So instead of reconstructing the dam the rulers called on the citizens to serve their city with greater efforts: they were to drink more water.

Water drinking festivals were organized. Drinking

squads patrolled the streets. The good citizen was seen at all times sipping from a glass of water in his hand. Medals were given to those who consumed large quantities. It's surprising what well-intentioned and public-spirited individuals can do on such occasions. One man drank fifty gallons of water each week for three weeks running before he drowned internally. He asked to be buried in a bath. There was much washing of the person and of possessions. People whose curtains were not constantly dripping could expect to have their windows broken by groups of young pioneers who were called The Water Babies. As the whole city was damp and as people went about in clothes that had been laundered to shreds and slept in damp beds, there was a lot of influenza about. Newspapers published daily casualty lists. These showed great increases in the number of cases of pneumonia. People also suffered from water on the knee and on the brain. Because the doorsteps and streets were washed so often many people slipped and the casualty service had to deal with sprained ankles and broken legs and backs. Of course the wounded – who had already made the sacrifice – could no longer drink very much or wash very often. The burden fell more heavily on the rest.

About this time patriotic people began to set fire to their houses so that firemen could hose them down. Loyalists also burned public buildings such as galleries, museums and schools. Nothing could be allowed to impede the city's efforts. National security was at stake. We can confidently say that the people's morale was never higher. And it worked. The level of water behind the dam fell. This overwhelming argument was used against those few disruptive elements who asked whether there might not be an easier way to control the dam. The dam wall no longer trembled. Dissenters were taken to their cell windows and made to stare up at it and declare that it stood as

firm as a rock. Every day the media reminded the people
of the days when the dam had been called Old Palsied and
they had lived in fear of The Burst. Things were going
well. All the more reason, then, for the massive outbreak
of dropsy to come as such a severe blow to the regime.
This blow was followed by another: people began to
burst. The rulers even wondered if the people could hold
out. As the Governor looked from his window he saw
passers by fall over in the street and roll to the side of
houses and lie there for minutes at a time without drinking. Perhaps there were inherent weaknesses in the
national character. How could such a nation survive?

The Governor himself felt worn out by the struggle
against water. He decided to address the people – perhaps,
he told himself, for the last time. The Water Police
rounded up the survivors and assembled them on the main
square. The Governor was surprised at the smallness of
the crowd. If the people had not been so bloated he would
have seen that it was even smaller than he thought. As the
Governor spoke one or two exploded. A new illness had
broken out: a fever which heated the blood and so caused
the water to boil. Sufferers emitted large amounts of steam
and a high whistling scream from their ears, mouth, nose
and anus till their bodies burst. The Governor spoke with
great dignity, raising his voice over the screaming, blurp-
ing, plopping, pissing and exploding. 'Fellow citizens!
This morning the figures were delivered to my desk. The
level of water in the dam is now so low that – should any
of you survive – you will be assured of three whole years
without danger of a dam burst. What the future holds
beyond then we cannot tell, but these three years are safe
– no matter how much rain falls! Citizens I salute your
great victory! God bless us!' He then became over-heated
with patriotic fervour and began to boil. He screamed and
emitted a cloud of steam. The crowd had counted up to

five before he exploded. As spring rainclouds gathered on the hills Water Police went among the crowd using the new-fangled hose-and-pump contraptions that had recently been introduced to enable them to pump water down the gullet of those who, however willing, were unable to swallow any more.

I Could Not Say

I could not say to those gathered in ghettoes to be gassed
Or to the El Salvadorean woman whose son was scalped
    and blinded
By soldiers looking for info before they butchered him
It is wrong to fight
When the problem is simple why make the solution hard?
But when the problem is hard we need a simple solution

Soldiers who fought the SS in Europe were sent to Africa
    to fight freedom fighters
The freedom fighters called the soldiers murderers
Soon the freedom fighters were honoured and entered
    into the councils of nations
So the soldiers were murderers?
No the regimental histories were not rewritten or medals
    taken from showcases
The soldiers were not murderers but merely instruments
Those who are instruments turn into beasts as the history
    of great follies makes clear

Too many are willing to squeeze triggers – pull levers –
    press buttons
And be instruments
That is why the rest of us are at the mercy of beasts
When enemies go to war it is too late to say it is wrong to
    fight
It must be said in peace
If you arm for war you make yourselves instruments and
    soon you will commit the great follies of beasts
You will murder the whimpering child – the dazed old –
    and the generations between
They are all as innocent as you
To spare you this hard fate there is a simple solution

It is better to kill your parents and wipe the blood from
your hands on their grey heads than kill old people
you have not seen

It is better to kill your child and wander the streets with
its blood on your hands than kill children you have
never heard cry

In this way you will keep your innocence

And there are even simpler ways to keep it

Bows and arrows are beyond human understanding –
riddles set by devils to astound gods

But nuclear weapons are simple and may easily be
understood

The Window

The bombardment and flushing-out had ended some days ago. The bombardiers were walking in the ruined town. Broken bits of buildings stuck up from the piles of rubble. The town looked like the fossilized graveyard of a herd of giant prehistoric reptiles.

They went into one of the ruined houses. One wall still stood. It was three storeys high. It was covered with the wallpapers and paints of several rooms. The joist holes for the floors and staircases were as neat as rows of bullet holes. Fireplaces still clung to it. The other walls, the floors and the roof were heaped on the ground to one side where the blast had blown them. The doors were gone from the hinges. There was a smell of damp dust and of acrid smoke from fires survivors had lit in some of the other ruins.

In the wall one window was left. It wasn't even cracked. A woman stood on a box in front of it and cleaned the glass. She had a rag and she'd filled an old plastic basin – the rim was badly chipped – at the emergency watertank on the square.

She wore bottle-green ankle-socks over her stockings, a dark mauve skirt, a grey jumper and a dark overcoat with large flat ugly buttons and a skimpy mottled bit of velveteen at the collar. Under the overcoat she wore an apron – pale green with blue zigzags. Round her neck there was a tooth-check scarf.

The woman saw the bombardiers. She stopped cleaning the window. As there were only three bombardiers she thought they were marauders. They would harm her. She raised her hands. One of them held the sopping rag. It dripped. The box didn't wobble.

The bombardiers stared at her. One of them gave a

quick reassuring wave. His hand rose no higher than his shoulder. The woman took the wave as an order to go on working. She thanked the bombardiers with two sharp syllables in her own language and gave an awkward but courtly little bow.

She turned her back on the bombardiers and went on cleaning the window. She began to jabber. Her voice was rather loud – as if she were talking to someone over her shoulder. That's how she'd shouted to her daughter or a neighbour before the house was ruined.

One bombardier asked the others 'Why clean a window in a ruin?'

Another asked 'What's she saying?'

Their voices were low. The first bombardier said 'She's saying it wasn't me. Had nothing to do with it. Didn't know what was going on.'

The bombardiers had a few hours off while the battery was rested. They walked on like tourists inspecting the ruins. They came to a low wall and sat on it. They'd drunk beer at the canteen tent. The day was sunny and still.

'Why?'

In the far distance an army lorry's wheels began to churn in mud.

'Mad. Thinks she's still at home with the family.'

'It was her house. She's getting on with minding the home.'

'It's where she worked. Thinks she's got to get it clean or the missuss'll sack her. Fall behind with the rent. Get chuck out.'

'The day our mum was bombed she swep the floor, hung the mat out to dry – the firehoses'd soaked it – boarded up the wall and cooked tea on our primus. My brother had to sit at the kitchen table and do his home-work. Wiped the brick-dust off his exercise book. His teacher rowed him out for being mucky.'

'When a cathedral's bombed there's always one window left standing.'

'A cathedral's got lots of windows. One of 'em's bound to survive. Same with towns. You send so many shells in you think only the worms are happy. Then some bastard crawls out of the ground. Same with soldiers and dugouts. There's so many people some survive.'

During the following days the incident was talked of a few times in the battery. The medical orderly said the woman was mad. But even if the shells and bombs had driven her mad, wasn't she doing something sane when she cleaned the window? The padre took it up in a sermon.

Some time later the three bombardiers walked through the ruins again.

'Let's look at the window.'

They couldn't find the house. Perhaps the wall had fallen down. They gave up looking and came on it by chance on their way back. One of them recognised the wallpaper in the top bedroom. They walked into the ground floor. There was the window. It was clean. Did the woman clean it every day? There was only one stain on it. Near the bottom some fluid had splashed across the glass. It had left a mark like the tongue of a cartoon fox.

The three bombardiers stared at the window for a minute.

'The old bird not here.'

'Should leave a tin of coffee on the ledge.'

'Too late. No time to come back. Battery moves tomorrow. All this'll be knock down when they rebuild. I hope the old crow – '

He stopped as the arm swung and the stone hit the glass. It shattered. The window had two panes. The bottom pane was shattered. A bombardier bent. He picked up a second stone – really a corner of a brick. He threw it at the top pane. It broke. Part of it shattered into the street. Part of it fell down and got hooked up on the jagged bits of the pane below – as if it was cutting the throat that ate it.

There was silence. There were no little fires burning in the ruins. The people had been moved out. A booby trap had blown off a soldier's foot.

None of the bombardiers spoke. War had turned them into expert watchers. They'd spied for targets and their eyes had wandered over the ruins they and others had made. Now perhaps they were waiting for the woman to come in screaming. Or to wander in with her chipped basin of water, see the broken window, kneel down and cry. Or shout. After the first shout she wouldn't risk cursing them. She'd curse the ruins. Or pray. Or mutter to herself as if she was telling the rubble how she'd lost her children. Or just say over and over in her strange language the word for hunger.

The woman didn't come. The bombardiers stood in silence for five minutes – a long time in a break in a war. Then they went away.

To them for a few days war seemed a little more decent.

You Are the First Generation

Each generation before us had a heaven
The miserable of the earth would be fed and clothed and
    the mighty stripped naked of power
So misery was borne on earth and scant happiness
    sacrificed
For joy in a place which did not exist in eternity on a
    calendar that began with an event that did not take
    place
But if the superstitious had not hoped for heaven the
    rulers would not have feared hell
They would have fallen on the people like wild beasts
Without illusions all would have perished
From illusions came understanding and truth – as always
In the flames heretics howled the ugly imprecations
That Newton refracted in prisms and found five laws
There was no god but he walked among us

Now we have made the machines and a thousand suns
    stand over the night and the darkness of day
Illusions no longer bring happiness or make us do good
If we believe we do not believe as the old believers
    believed
If we believe in their god we turn into devils
All gods are destroyed by their worshippers' miracles
We have killed god: he is possessed with devils
The calendar has fallen into its own emptiness
And what is true of religion is true of politics – as always
We are the first generation without a heaven
We howl because we're in heaven
We are armageddon
Satan presides at our judgement

Already there are signs
The rich richer – the poor poorer
Children mortgaged for generations with the debts of
    their fathers
Aristocratic skeletons resurrected with bone grafts
Frenzy at little wars
Confusion and slippery management
More prisoners – calls for capital punishment
In an age of technology these things are among the first
    signs of fascism
Then there are nuclear weapons: we arm the figure in the
    mirror and fear it
There is no devil but he walks among us

To understand our state consider a simple creature
The startled hare in the torchlight
Erect ears as tall as the rest of its body
Each strand of fur as rigid as a rifle barrel
Each whisker as tense as a trigger-finger
The eyes as concentrated as two nails in a coffin
For a moment it eavesdrops on death
And chews
Then bolts over the grass in every direction between
    cradle and grave
And chews
The jaws move at their own pace as if they did not belong
    to the leaping body
They work as fast as bobbins knitting a shroud
It is the delirious gossip of one who sleeps
Or the ticks in a clockwork mask on a corpse
Before the hunter came it learned: eat or die
It repeats its lesson to the gun that knocks it in the air
It chews
And somersaults into the grave with a mouthful of grass

Can you survive your strengths?

Illusions have given you armies and crafts – factories
      farms hovels and citadels – injustice from which
          you made noble laws and errors which served
              you as the highest truth

You were idols of clay with feet of marble and danced on
      water

It was all god would allow you to do – he coveted the
      earth and its fruits

God was devious and the oracles spoke riddles

So heretics were confused and foolish: but they could not
      lie

You are the first generation able to lie

The machines have told you the truth: they do not covet
      or riddle

Illusions will not save you from the death lies bring

Learn to be human

Only humans can live with machines

Only devils can live with god

Machines are not devious and they cannot forgive

Nor can they change but you are not made in their image

To justify your crimes you boast you stand in the ranks
      of angels

To excuse your brutalities you claim the birthright of
      beasts

Now you must learn to be human

Or you will somersault into the grave with a mouthful of
      grass

The Swallows

At five in the morning the flock of swallows flew down
     to perch on the little boat
In rows on the railing and ropes preening and shrilly
     chittering
Their heads turn with a series of quick little jerks as if
     they worked on ratchets
Some burrow their beaks into their backs – some
          suddenly shoot out a wing – a fan hit open or razor
               slash – and run the edge through their beaks
The edge is marked like a samurai pennant with little
     white squares and their eyes are set in a black band
They preen as insistently as if they gnawed their own
     flesh
When they stop their faces are blank
The pin-thin beaks jut from the downy round heads like
     pivots on top of globes
For ten minutes the mob chivvies and squeaks and vies
     for places though no place is more sheltered than
          another or gives a better view
They jerk as awkwardly as puppets tangled in their
     strings
The noise! – madmen let loose in a belfry or condemned
     fighting their executioners
And suddenly they are silent – all at the same instant
Not one sound or movement
Not even a feather ruffles
They are not asleep
After five minutes one slightly cocks its head – one looks
     down at its feet – one opens and shuts its silent beak
Then they are still
No wind or wave or traffic

look before them as if each gazed at the same thing
    though many perch back to back
And minutes pass
There is a photograph taken inside a room that's said to
    show the last man being shot in the second world
        war: he falls back from a sunny window
            dropping his gun
In every war someone is the last to be killed
In time someone will be the last to be killed by any
    weapon
Then there will be silence – a great peace will grow and
    we can imagine how it will change as time passes
Already memorials to that man or woman stand in our
    streets and birds come to rest on them
Suddenly the swallows rise in a fast sweep and swirl
    down the wind tunnel over the river
There is one fading screech
And I am left with the bare rail and the ropes

[Notes]

1 *Gotcha!* (The Media, the Government and the Falklands
Crisis) by Robert Harris. Faber & Faber, 1983. p. 36.
(Reprinted by permission of the Peters, Fraser and
Dunlop Group.)
2 *Task Force: The Falklands War, 1982* by Martin
Middlebrook. Penguin Books, 1985. p. 282. (Reprinted
by permission of Penguin Books.)
3 *Gotcha!* p. 46.
4 *Task Force*, p. 165.
5 *Task Force*, p. 231.

Methuen Modern Plays
include work by

Jean Anouilh
John Arden
Margaretta D'Arcy
Peter Barnes
Sebastian Barry
Brendan Behan
Dermot Bolger
Edward Bond
Bertolt Brecht
Howard Brenton
Anthony Burgess
Simon Burke
Jim Cartwright
Caryl Churchill
Noël Coward
Lucinda Coxon
Sarah Daniels
Nick Darke
Nick Dear
Shelagh Delaney
David Edgar
David Eldridge
Dario Fo
Michael Frayn
John Godber
Paul Godfrey
David Greig
John Guare
Peter Handke
David Harrower
Jonathan Harvey
Iain Heggie
Declan Hughes
Terry Johnson
Sarah Kane
Charlotte Keatley
Barrie Keeffe
Howard Korder

Robert Lepage
Stephen Lowe
Doug Lucie
Martin McDonagh
John McGrath
Terrence McNally
David Mamet
Patrick Marber
Arthur Miller
Mtwa, Ngema & Simon
Tom Murphy
Phyllis Nagy
Peter Nichols
Joseph O'Connor
Joe Orton
Louise Page
Joe Penhall
Luigi Pirandello
Stephen Poliakoff
Franca Rame
Mark Ravenhill
Philip Ridley
Reginald Rose
David Rudkin
Willy Russell
Jean-Paul Sartre
Sam Shepard
Wole Soyinka
Shelagh Stephenson
C. P. Taylor
Theatre de Complicite
Theatre Workshop
Sue Townsend
Judy Upton
Timberlake Wertenbaker
Roy Williams
Victoria Wood

Methuen Contemporary Dramatists
include

Peter Barnes (three volumes)
Sebastian Barry
Edward Bond (six volumes)
Howard Brenton
  (two volumes)
Richard Cameron
Jim Cartwright
Caryl Churchill (two volumes)
Sarah Daniels (two volumes)
Nick Darke
David Edgar (three volumes)
Ben Elton
Dario Fo (two volumes)
Michael Frayn (two volumes)
Paul Godfrey
John Guare
Peter Handke
Jonathan Harvey
Declan Hughes
Terry Johnson (two volumes)
Bernard-Marie Koltès
David Lan
Bryony Lavery
Doug Lucie
David Mamet (three volumes)

Martin McDonagh
Duncan McLean
Anthony Minghella
  (two volumes)
Tom Murphy (four volumes)
Phyllis Nagy
Anthony Nielsen
Philip Osment
Louise Page
Joe Penhall
Stephen Poliakoff
  (three volumes)
Christina Reid
Philip Ridley
Willy Russell
Ntozake Shange
Sam Shepard (two volumes)
Wole Soyinka (two volumes)
David Storey (three volumes)
Sue Townsend
Michel Vinaver (two volumes)
Michael Wilcox
David Wood (two volumes)
Victoria Wood

Methuen World Classics
include

Jean Anouilh (two volumes)
John Arden (two volumes)
Arden & D'Arcy
Brendan Behan
Aphra Behn
Bertolt Brecht (six volumes)
Büchner
Bulgakov
Calderón
Čapek
Anton Chekhov
Noël Coward (seven volumes)
Eduardo De Filippo
Max Frisch
John Galsworthy
Gogol
Gorky
Harley Granville Barker
  (two volumes)
Henrik Ibsen (six volumes)
Lorca (three volumes)

Marivaux
Mustapha Matura
David Mercer (two volumes)
Arthur Miller (five volumes)
Molière
Musset
Peter Nichols (two volumes)
Clifford Odets
Joe Orton
A. W. Pinero
Luigi Pirandello
Terence Rattigan
  (two volumes)
W. Somerset Maugham
  (two volumes)
August Strindberg
  (three volumes)
J. M. Synge
Ramón del Valle-Inclán
Frank Wedekind
Oscar Wilde

Methuen Classical Greek Dramatists

Aeschylus Plays: One
(Persians, Seven Against Thebes, Suppliants,
Prometheus Bound)

Aeschylus Plays: Two
(Oresteia: Agamemnon, Libation-Bearers, Eumenides)

Aristophanes Plays: One
(Acharnians, Knights, Peace, Lysistrata)

Aristophanes Plays: Two
(Wasps, Clouds, Birds, Festival Time, Frogs)

Aristophanes & Menander: New Comedy
(Women in Power, Wealth, The Malcontent,
The Woman from Samos)

Euripides Plays: One
(Medea, The Phoenician Women, Bacchae)

Euripides Plays: Two
(Hecuba, The Women of Troy, Iphigeneia at Aulis,
Cyclops)

Euripides Plays: Three
(Alkestis, Helen, Ion)

Euripides Plays: Four
(Elektra, Orestes, Iphigeneia in Tauris)

Euripides Plays: Five
(Andromache, Herakles' Children, Herakles)

Euripides Plays: Six
(Hippolytos, Suppliants, Rhesos)

Sophocles Plays: One
(Oedipus the King, Oedipus at Colonus, Antigone)

Sophocles Plays: Two
(Ajax, Women of Trachis, Electra, Philoctetes)

Methuen Student Editions

John Arden	*Serjeant Musgrave's Dance*
Alan Ayckbourn	*Confusions*
Aphra Behn	*The Rover*
Edward Bond	*Lear*
Bertolt Brecht	*The Caucasian Chalk Circle*
	Life of Galileo
	Mother Courage and her Children
Anton Chekhov	*The Cherry Orchard*
Caryl Churchill	*Top Girls*
Shelagh Delaney	*A Taste of Honey*
John Galsworthy	*Strife*
Robert Holman	*Across Oka*
Henrik Ibsen	*A Doll's House*
Charlotte Keatley	*My Mother Said I Never Should*
Bernard Kops	*Dreams of Anne Frank*
Federico García Lorca	*Blood Wedding*
	The House of Bernarda Alba
	(bilingual edition)
John Marston	*The Malcontent*
Willy Russell	*Blood Brothers*
Wole Soyinka	*Death and the King's Horseman*
August Strindberg	*The Father*
J. M. Synge	*The Playboy of the Western World*
Oscar Wilde	*The Importance of Being Earnest*
Tennessee Williams	*A Streetcar Named Desire*
Timberlake Wertenbaker	*Our Country's Good*